$25.00

665954

Blue Dog
Speaks

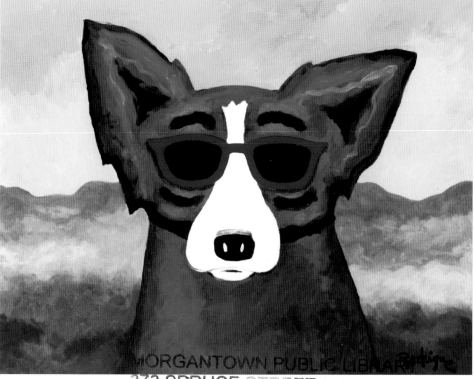

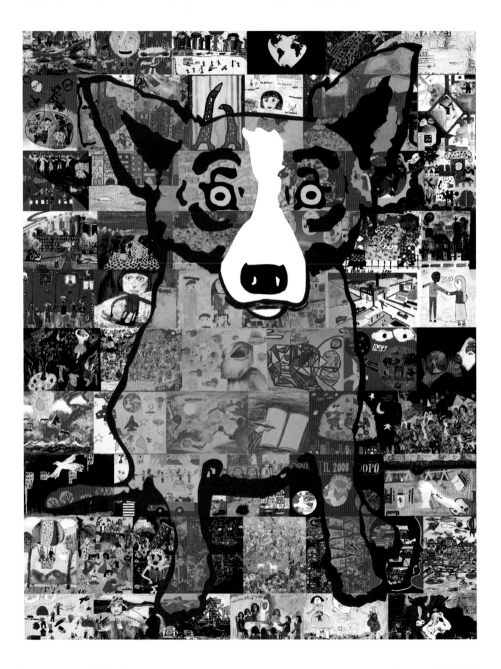

Blue Dog Speaks

George Rodrigue

STERLING

New York / London
www.sterlingpublishing.com

Blue Dog works

on half title: Shades of Hollywood

opposite title page: Honesty

STERLING and the distinctive Sterling logo are registered trademarks
of Sterling Publishing Co., Inc.

Library of Congress Cataloging-in-Publication Data
Rodrigue, George
    Blue dog speaks / George Rodrigue
        p. cm.
    Includes index.
    ISBN 978-1-4027-5408-1
    1. Rodrigue, George—Themes, motives.   I. Title.
    ND237.R69A4   2008
    759.13—dc22
                                2008010206

10 9 8 7 6 5 4 3 2 1

Published by Sterling Publishing Co., Inc.
387 Park Avenue South, New York, NY 10016
© 2008 by George Rodrigue
Distributed in Canada by Sterling Publishing
c/o Canadian Manda Group, 165 Dufferin Street
Toronto, Ontario, Canada M6K 3H6
Distributed in the United Kingdom by GMC Distribution Services
Castle Place, 166 High Street, Lewes, East Sussex, England BN7 1XU
Distributed in Australia by Capricorn Link (Australia) Pty. Ltd.
P.O. Box 704, Windsor, NSW 2756, Australia

Printed in China

Sterling ISBN 978-1-4027-5408-1

For information about custom editions, special sales, premium
and corporate purchases, please contact Sterling Special Sales
Department at 800-805-5489 or specialsales@sterlingpublishing.com.

To Brother Edward Scanlan,
who threw me out of class for drawing

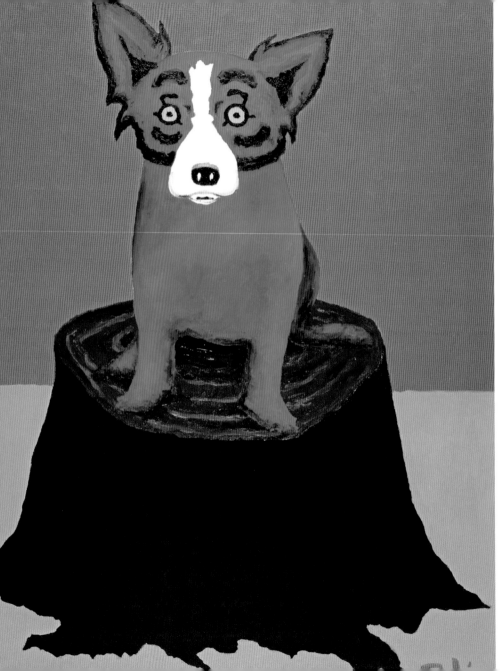

Speaking
on the
Stump

CONTENTS

INTRODUCTION

If I were to make a FAQ list, at the top would have to be, "How do you come up with the titles?" and "Do you know what you're going to paint before you start?"

Truth is I usually have *no idea* what the title or subject matter is going to be when I pick up the paintbrush. It's all about keeping things fresh. If I don't know exactly where I'm going with a painting, I have more fun; the creative process is more exciting.

These days, one thing I do know is that it will be a Blue Dog. When I began the series of Blue Dog paintings in 1984, I had no idea that they would consume the greater part of my life for over two decades. The original concept of a Blue Dog was not what it is today. The idea came from a Cajun childhood story that was brought over from France by the Acadians. It simply stated that if you were not good today, the *loup-garou* would get you tonight. I remember my mother relating this story many times to me as I was growing up. The legend said nothing about a dog or the color blue. But it did link this spooky werewolf creature to cemeteries and sugar cane fields and dark night skies. I thought that same sky would cast a blue-grey shade on the creature; and the red eyes of those early paintings removed any link to Tiffany, my studio dog-turned-model.

My early Blue Dog paintings were a reflection of this childhood idea and meant little beyond their connection to a ghost story. The titles, such as *Cosmos Dog*, *Missing My Master*, or *I Went to the Graveyard to Hide from the Blues,* reflected the dog's position on tombstones and under dark trees at midnight. The whole concept changed for me during an exhibition of my work in Los Angeles in the late 1980s when I overheard people call this wolfish-type *loup-garou* "Blue Dog."

Returning to my Louisiana studio, I painted Blue Dog images that reflected ideas in the present. I changed the eyes to yellow and dared to take the bayou legend out of the bayou! The titles were an important part of this transition.

Before the Blue Dog, the titles of my Cajun landscapes merely reflected a place, such as *Broussard's Barber Shop* or *Sugar Bridge Over Coulee*. They did not express a concept about contemporary life or add any extra insight to the work. But in these new paintings, I used the titles as a tool to convey further meaning. This Blue Dog could now travel in time and space away from Louisiana, away from the landscapes of the bayou, and into places where it had never gone before. I enhanced these visual ideas with titles such as *Right Place, Wrong Time* and *Tiffany Remembers the '70s,* and later more abstract concepts such as *All by Myself with My Happiness* and *You Would Think We Are the Same*. After twenty-five years of painting the Cajuns of the past, these new Blue Dog paintings became a vehicle for me to say things about *today*.

I feel like I'm on a journey to find an answer to each painting. Usually about halfway to completion (which could take anywhere from four hours to two weeks) a title and a concept evolve. From then on, I mold the painting to reinforce that title. Yet even though the title is important to the idea of the painting, an enigma—a sense of mystery—remains, and the painting invites the viewer to fill in the blanks according to his or her own needs and experiences.

A simple Blue Dog is the obvious visual subject of every painting. However, the title combines with the paint on the canvas to convey a deeper meaning: one that in the end rarely alludes to that animal we know as "dog," but instead provides insight—whether humorous or nostalgic or sad—into the human condition. I have always said, ever since my earliest Cajun landscapes and genre works, that my work is meant to make people stop and pause, to speculate and ponder. My hope is that this process allows the viewer to become an integral part of the work's meaning. In this book you will see a broad range of subjects and titles and ideas, and I hope it helps you understand the infinite concepts possible.

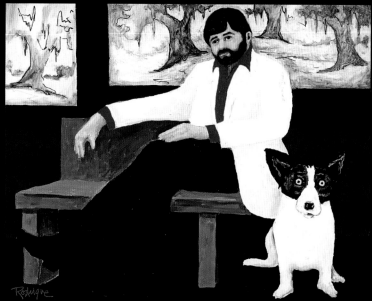

Blue Dog Speaks is the first book to emphasize my titles alongside the works. In previous books, the titles were relegated to small italicized lines or indexes—or worse, not included at all. The mere fact that this book gives the titles the same prominence and space as the paintings, gives the reader a new understanding of the titles' importance.

—George Rodrigue

Disco on Duclos

1

BoRN
on
the
BaYou

Dreaming of Evangeline

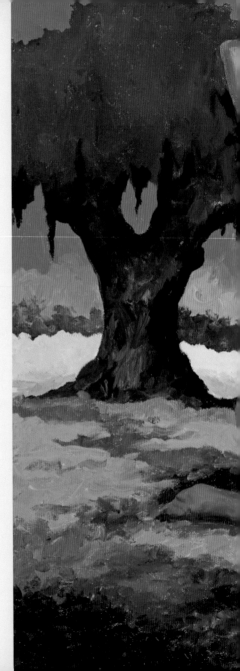

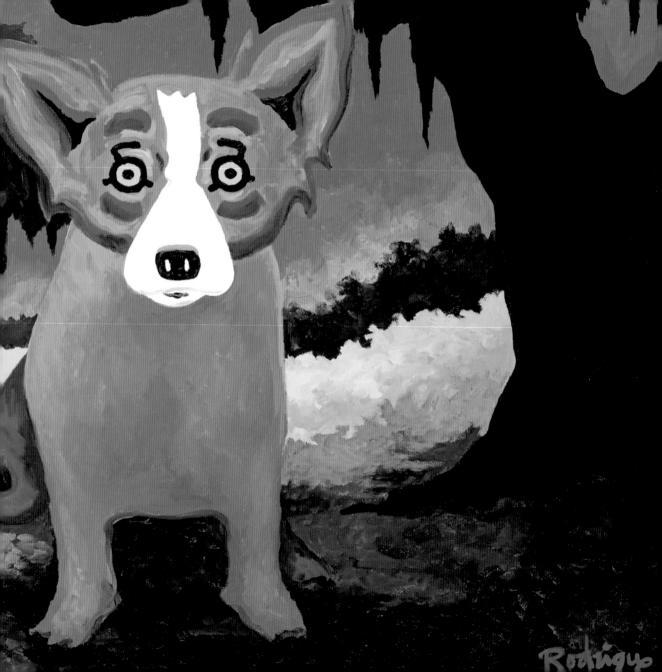

I Live By My ROOTS

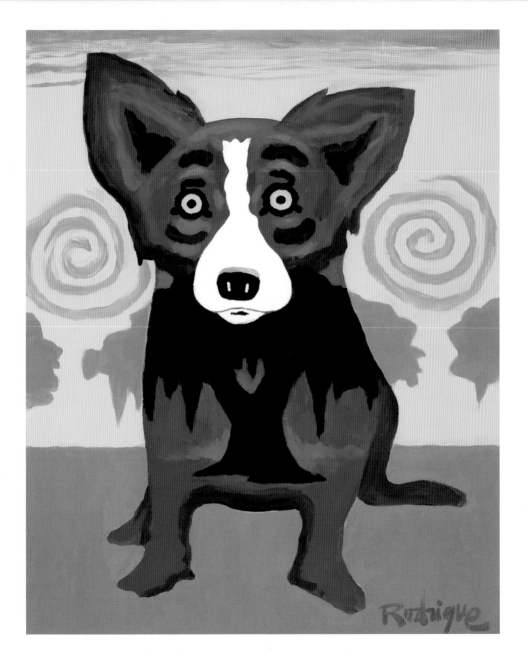

13

MY
AcaDian
HeritaGe

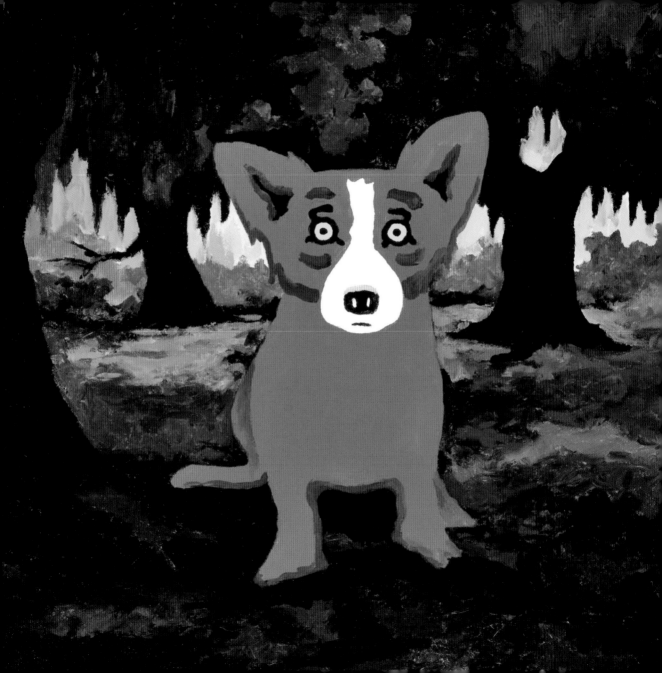

The

Tree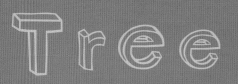

My

MaMa

Slept

Under

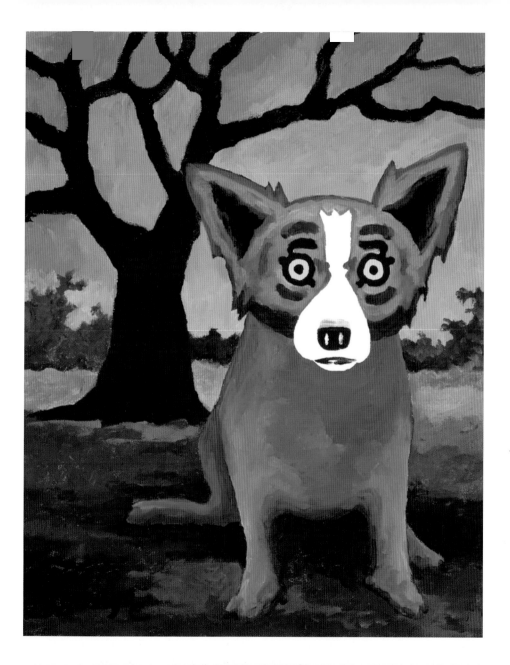

17

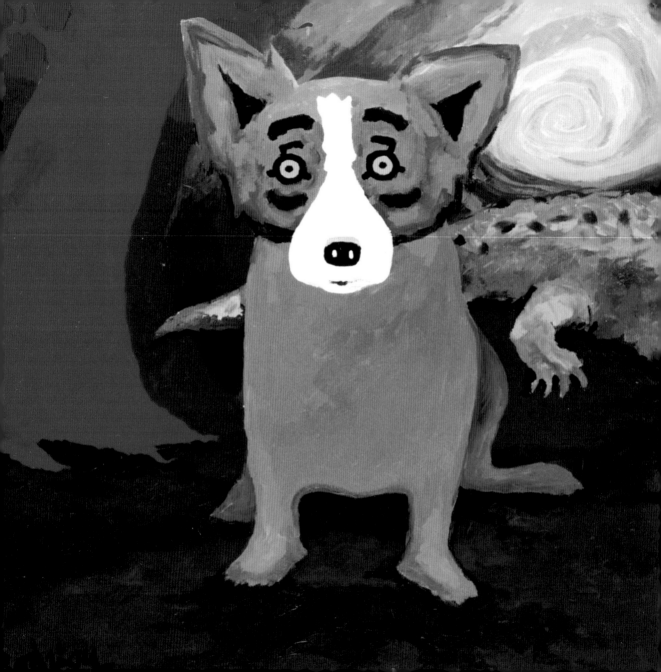

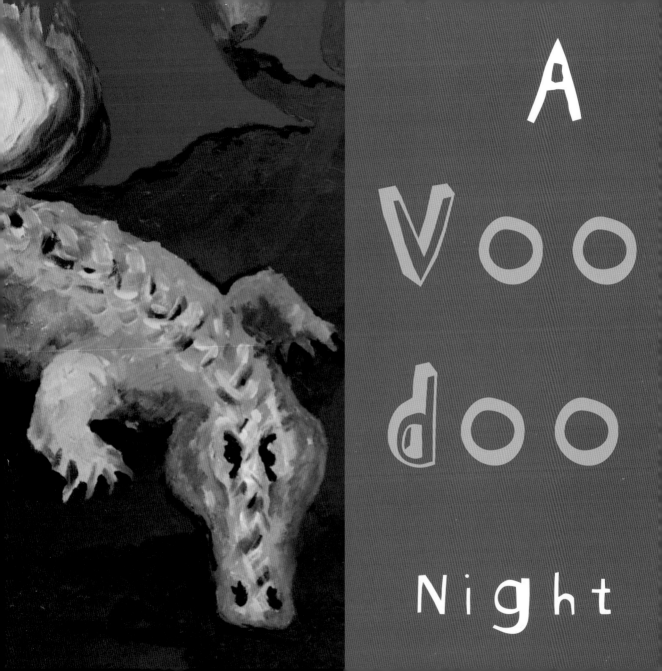

A Voo doo

Night

Tee

Paul's

HouSe

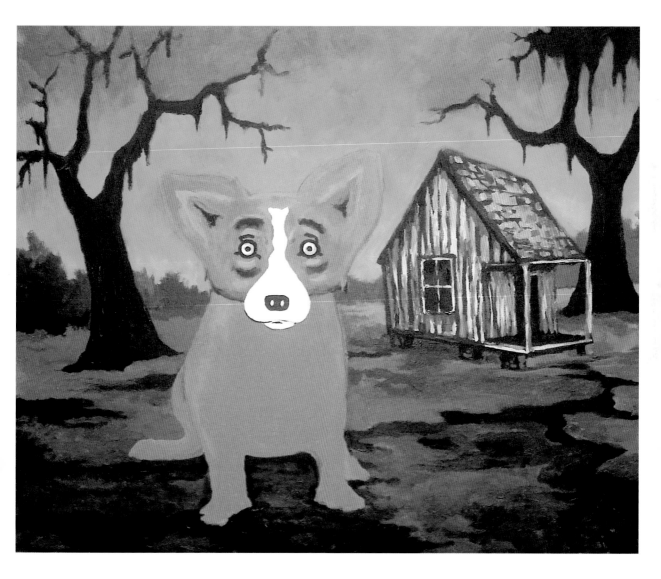

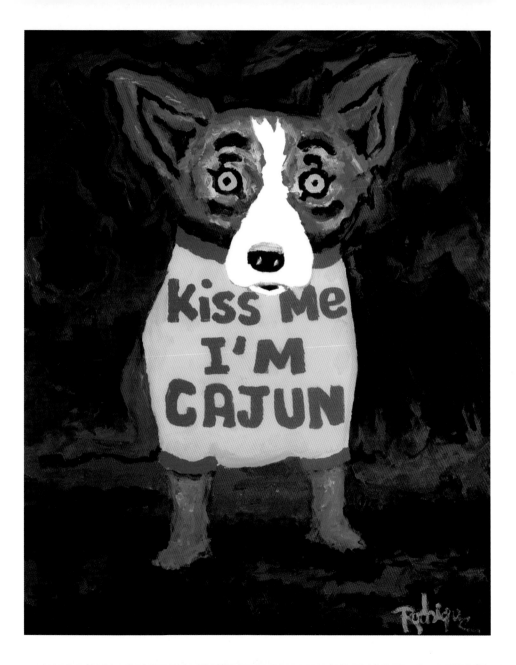

23

Come BAck and Ligten Ligh Up on My BluEs

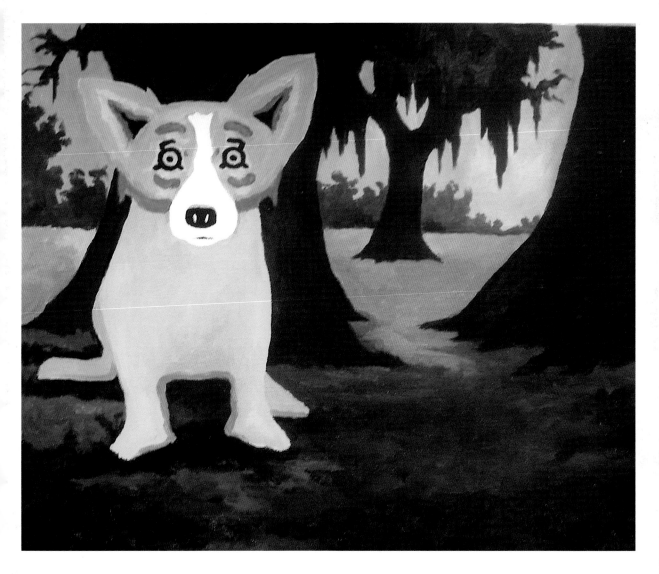

Paint

Me Back

Into

YouR

Life

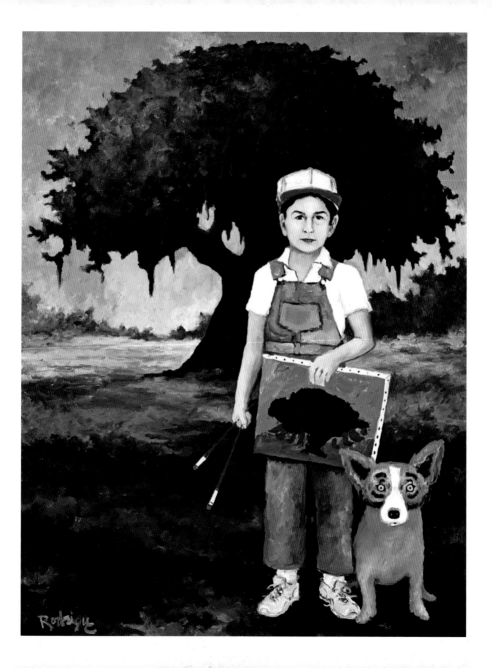

27

A

DoWn

Deep

Blue Midnight

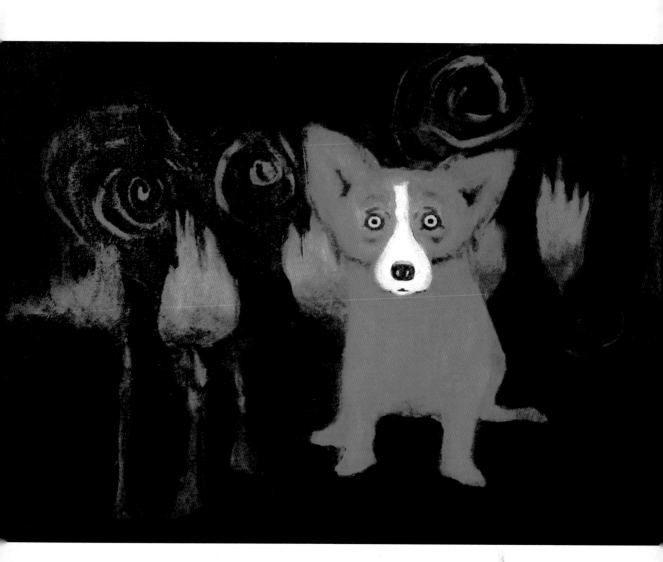

29

It's Greek to Me

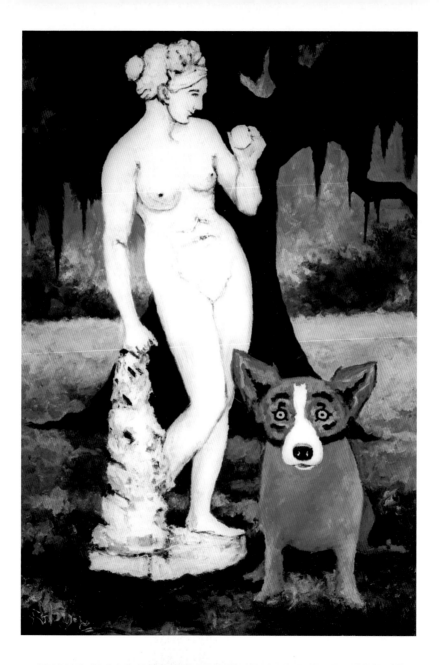

31

Again

I'm

Alone

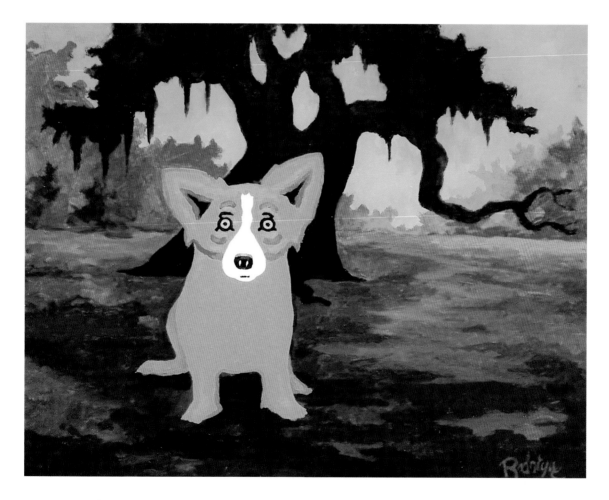

Take Five

Take Five

Take Five

Take Five

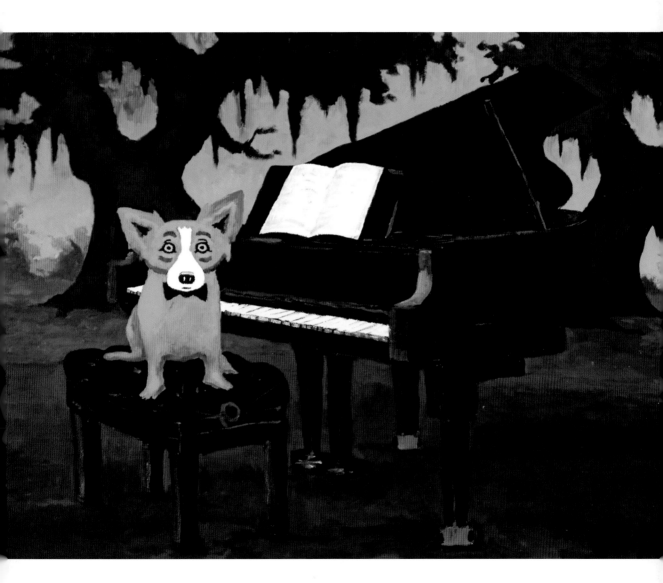

When She
Left Me
My

Blues

Got

Deeper

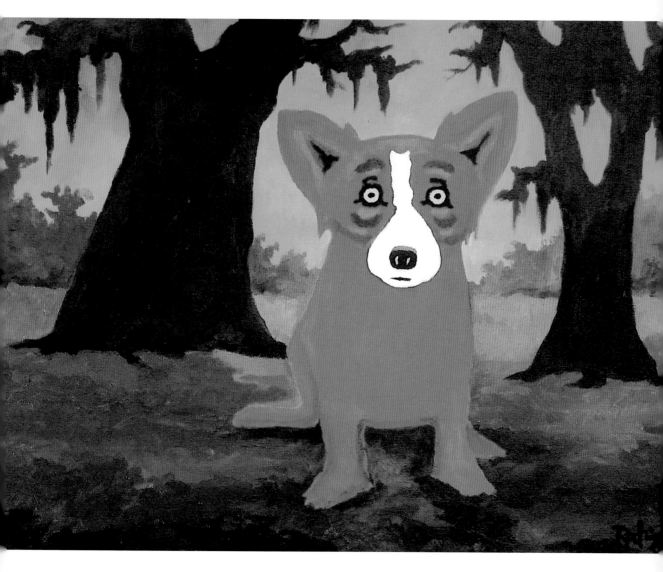

Valentino's Revenge

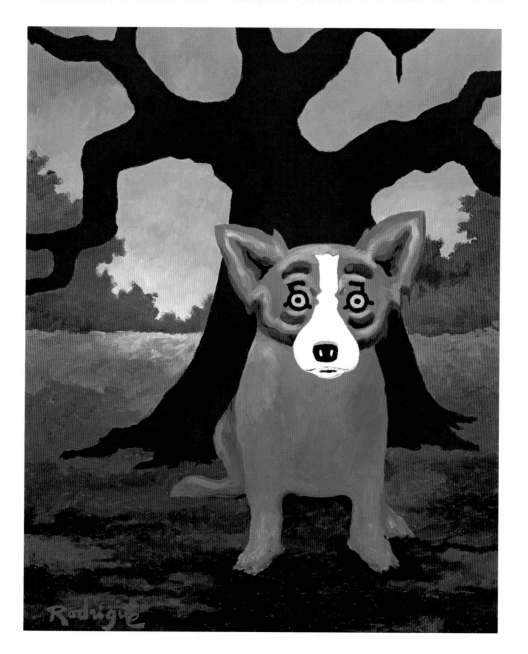

A Pack of Oak Groves

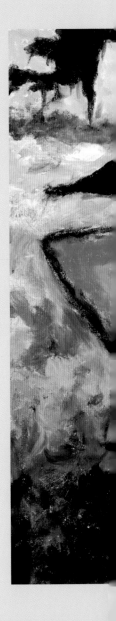

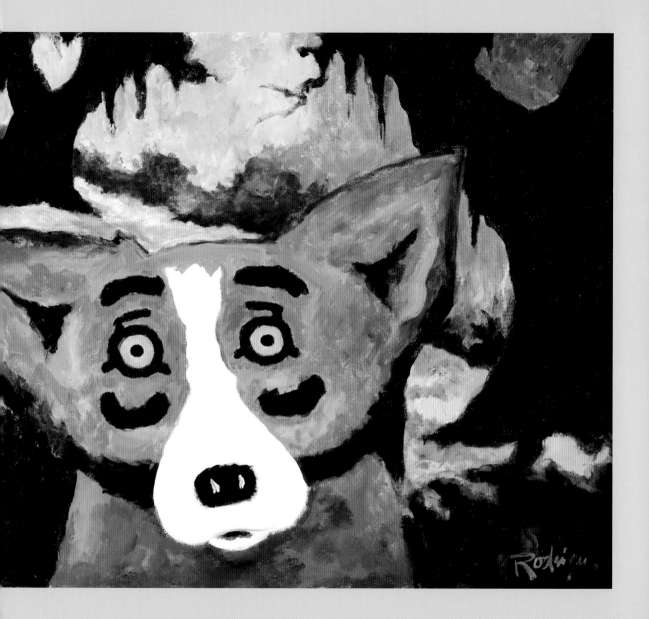

A Pack of Trees

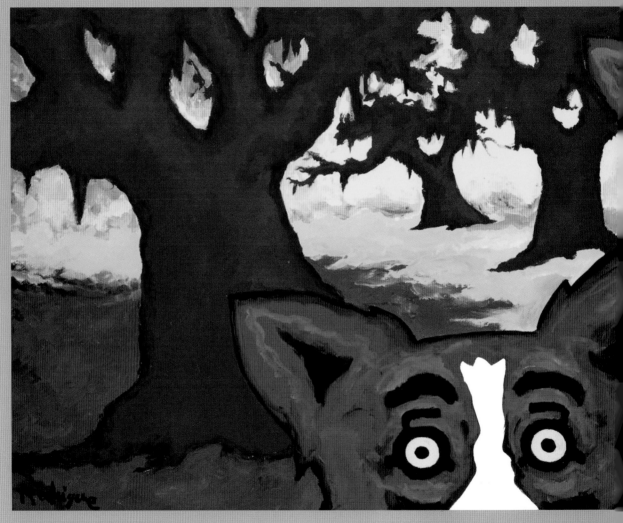

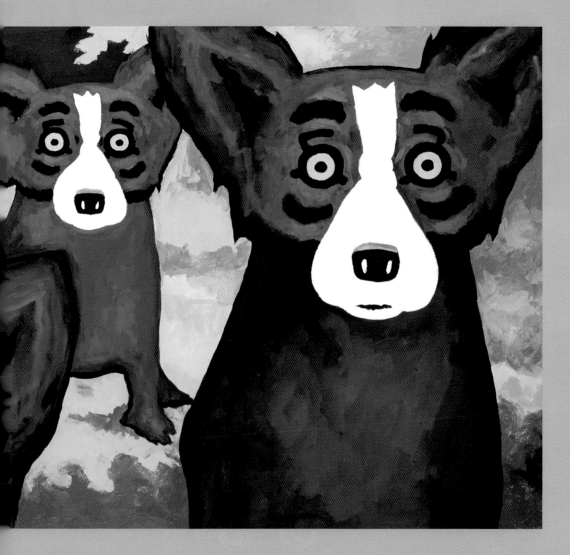

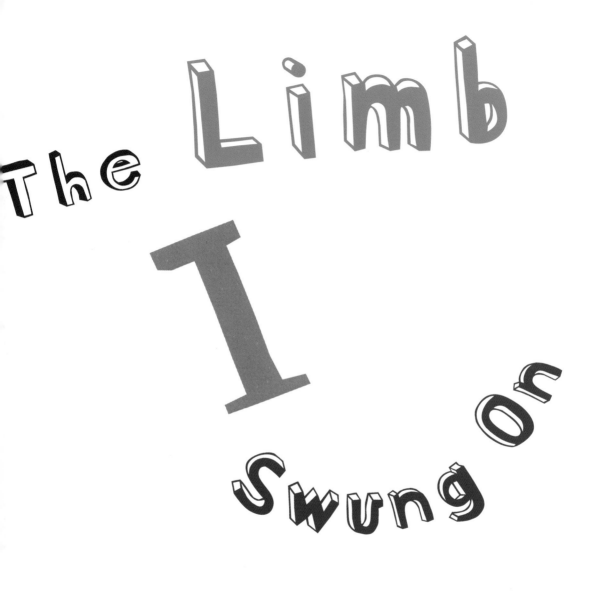

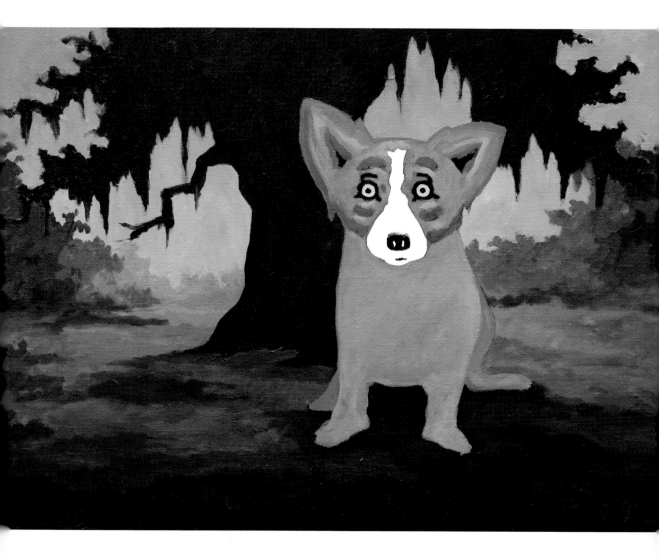

45

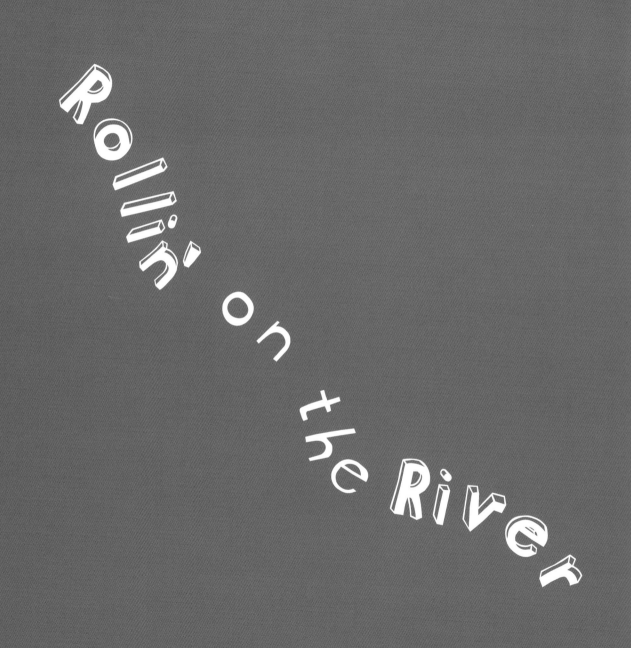

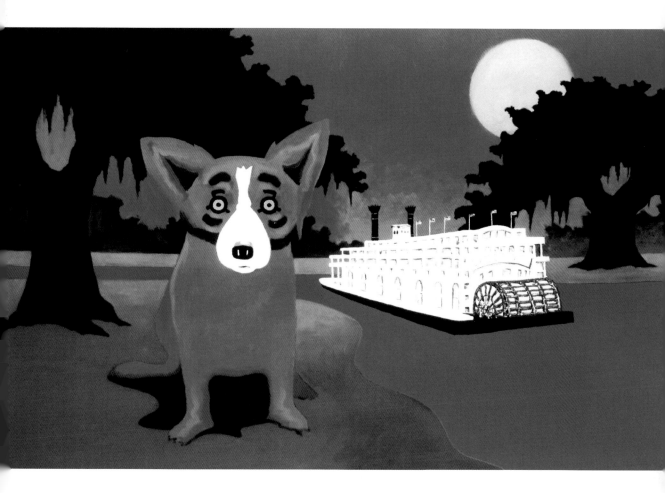

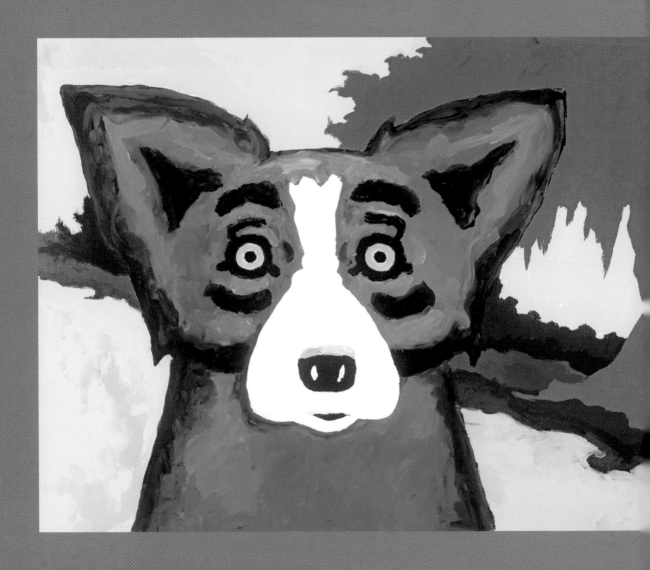

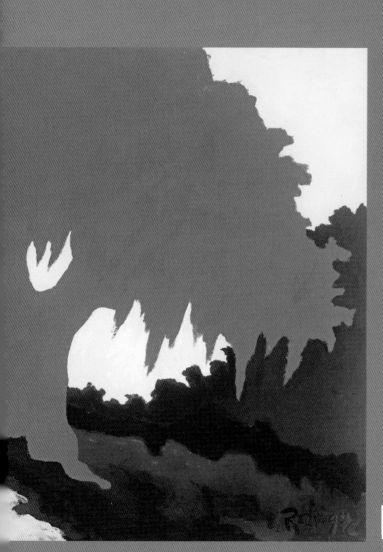

A Slice of Louisiana

Little Joe

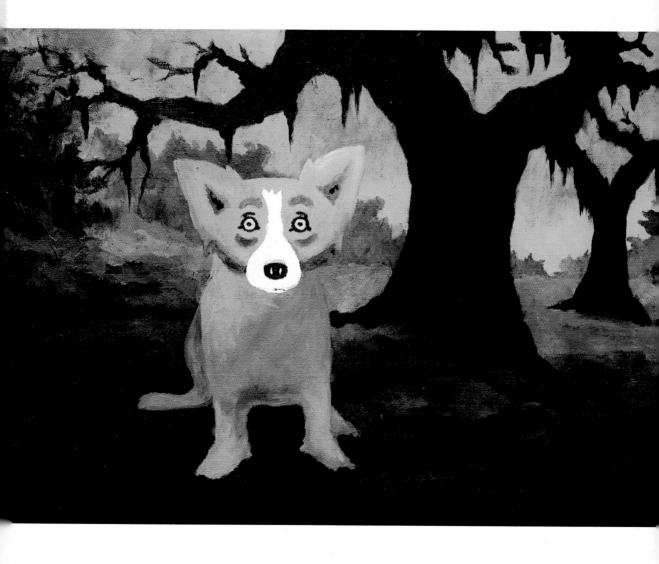

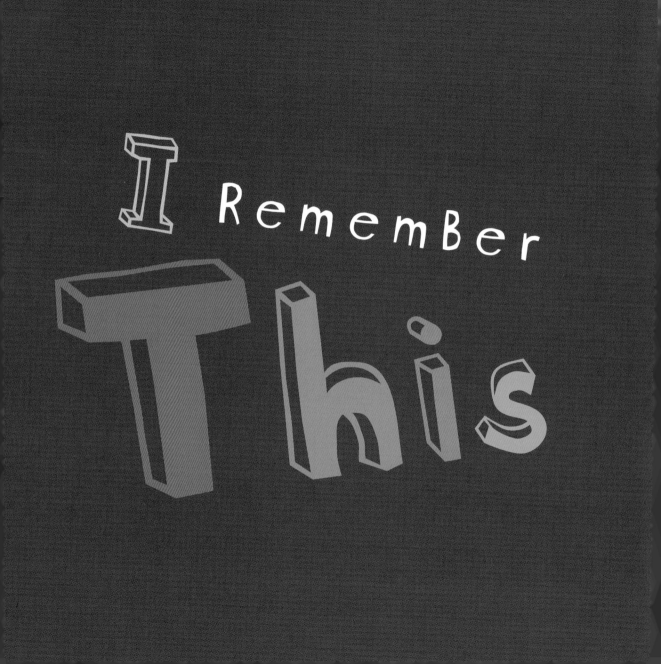

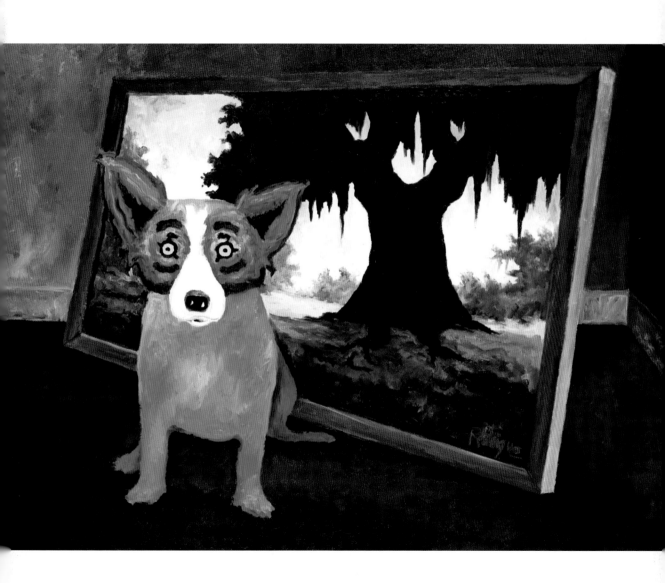

Take the Picture Now

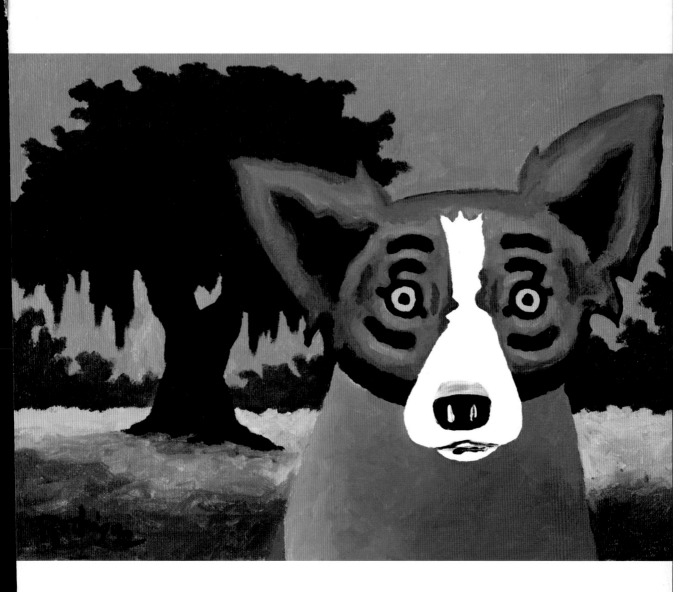

55

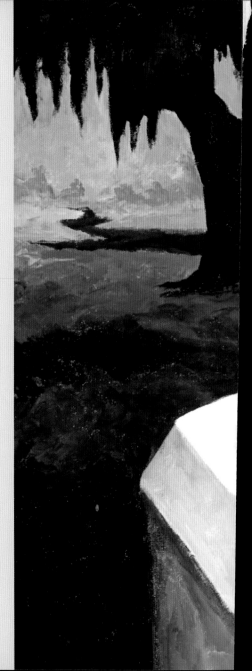

2

The
Other
SiDe

Resting Between the Trees

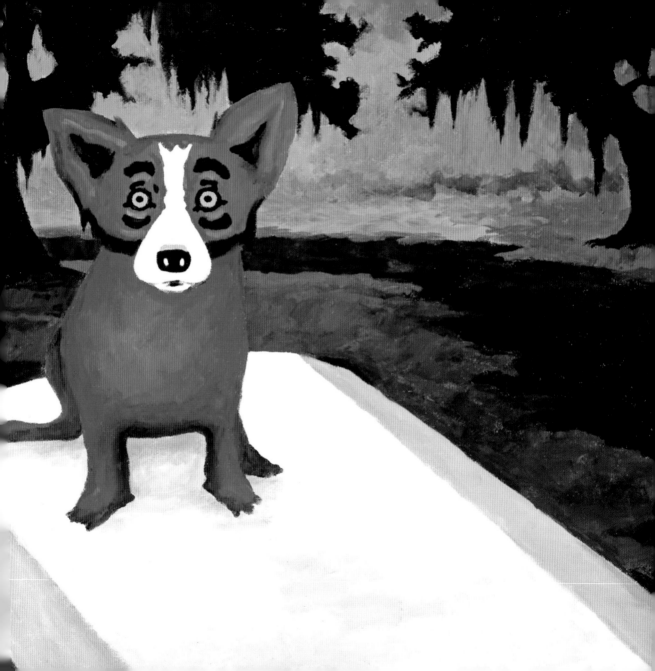

The

Re - Birth

of

TiffaNy

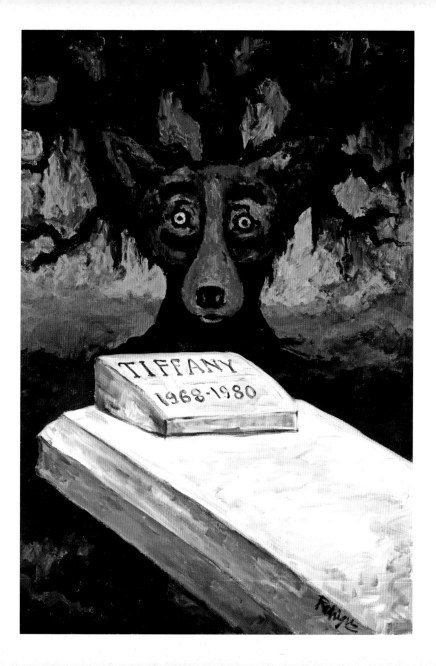

A
Novena
for Me

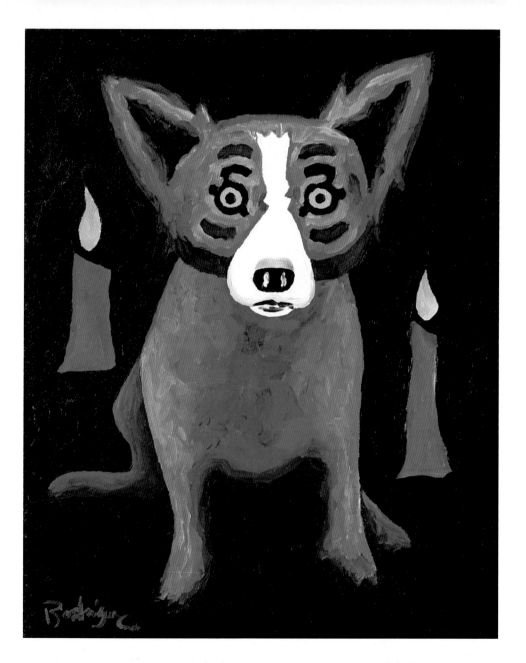

61

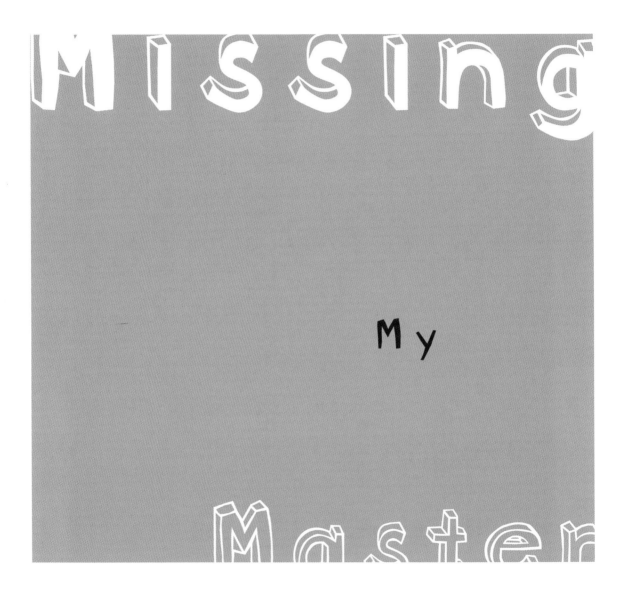

Missing

My

Master

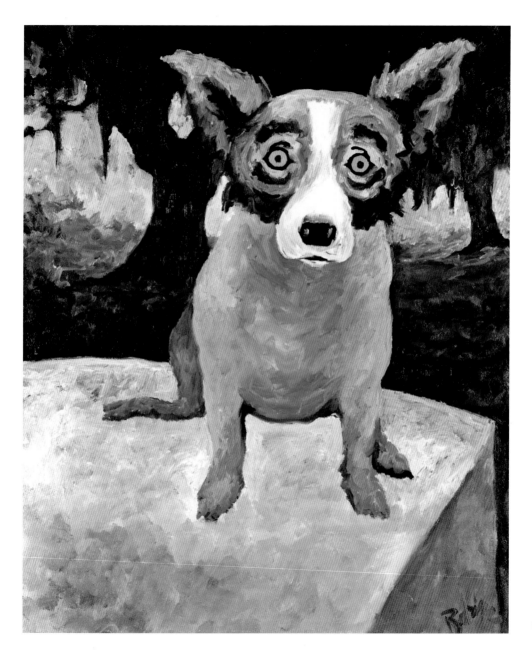

63

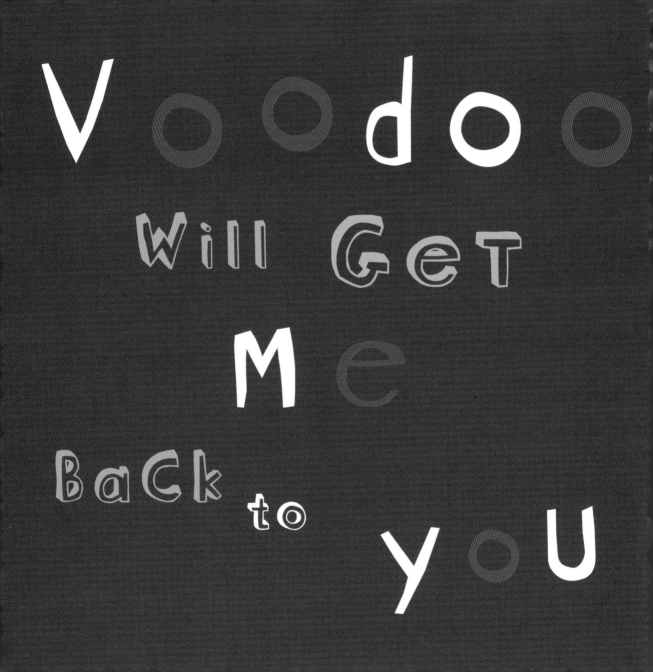

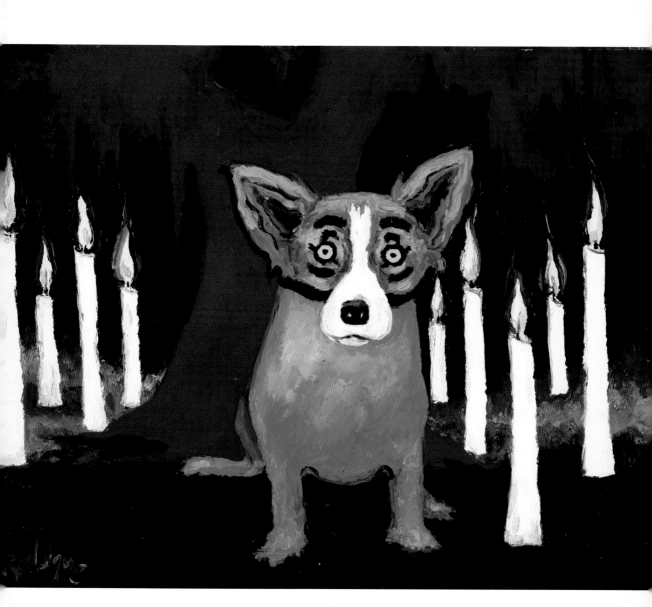

65

Don't GroW Grass on Me

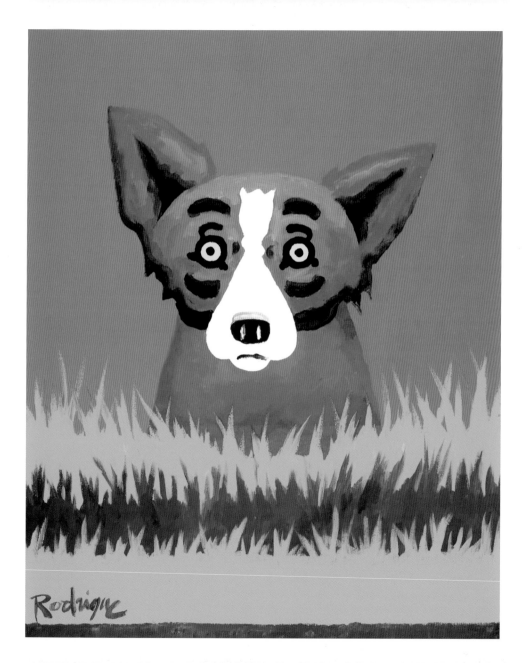

Rodrigue

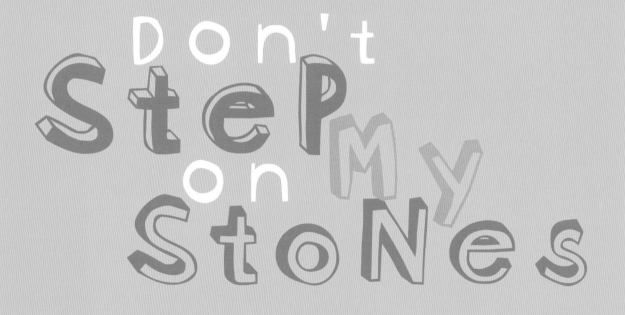

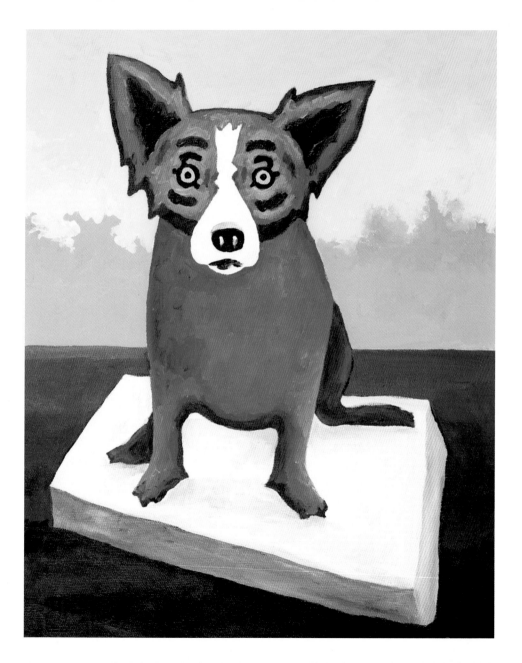

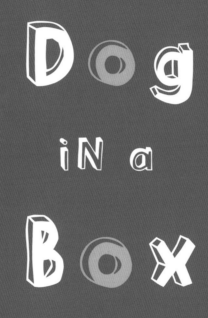

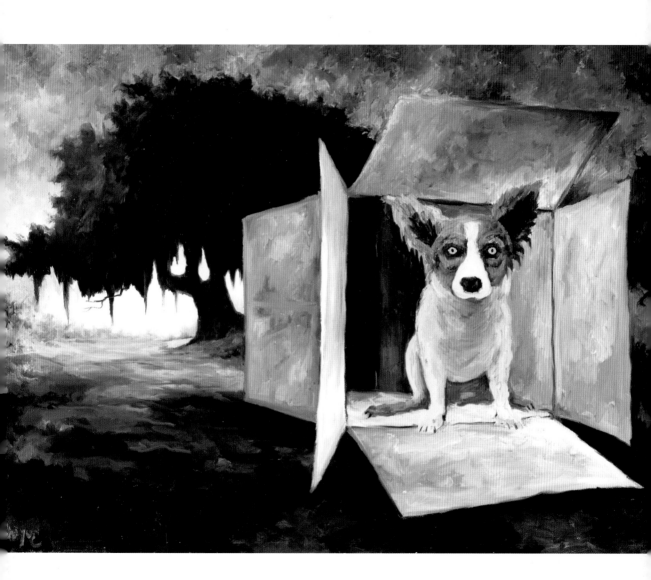

71

The Path of the Candles

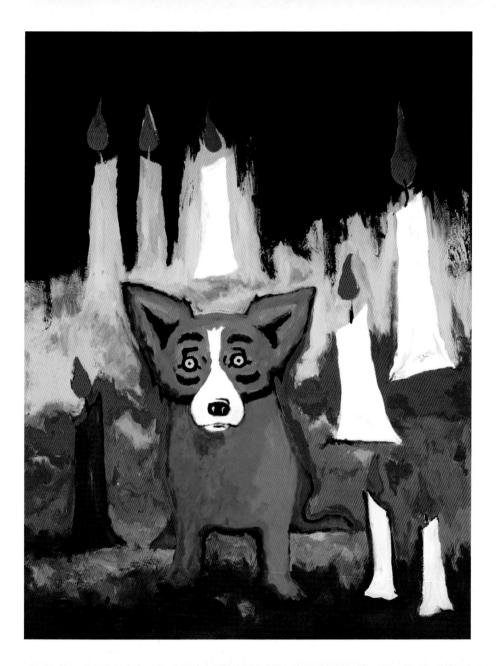

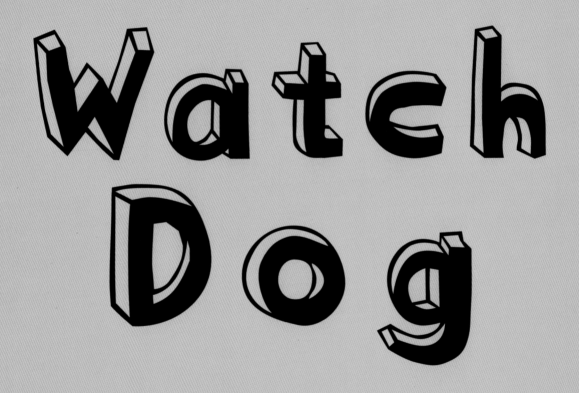

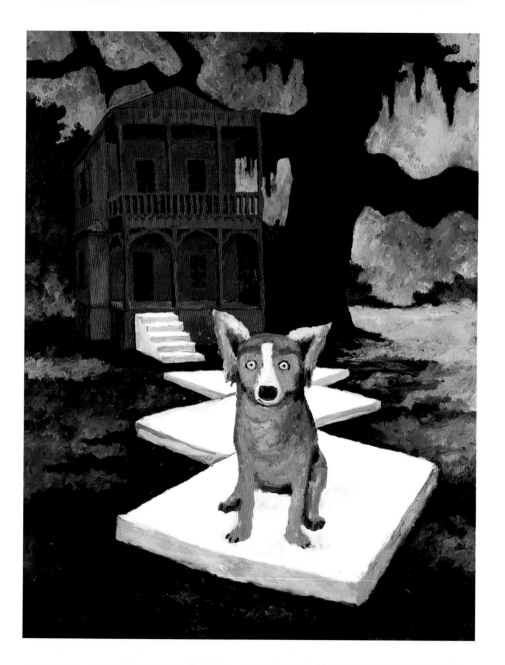

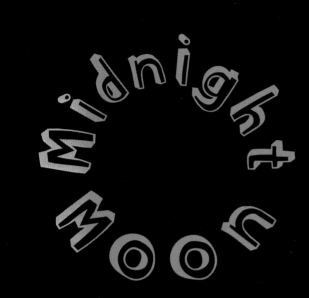

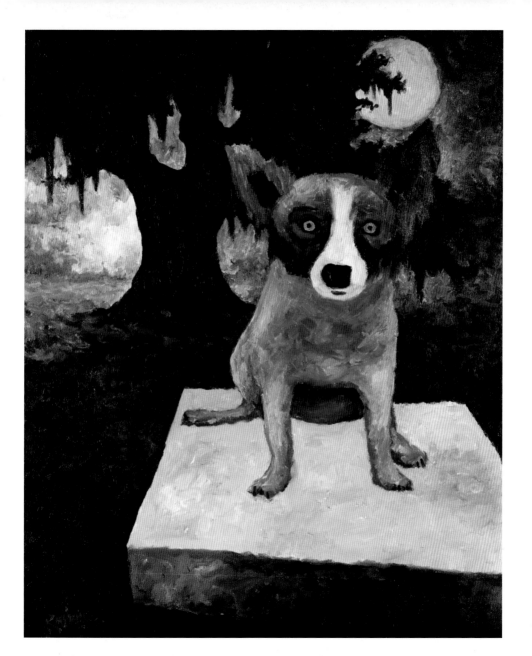

3
Pure
and
Simple

It's Your Turn to Make a Move

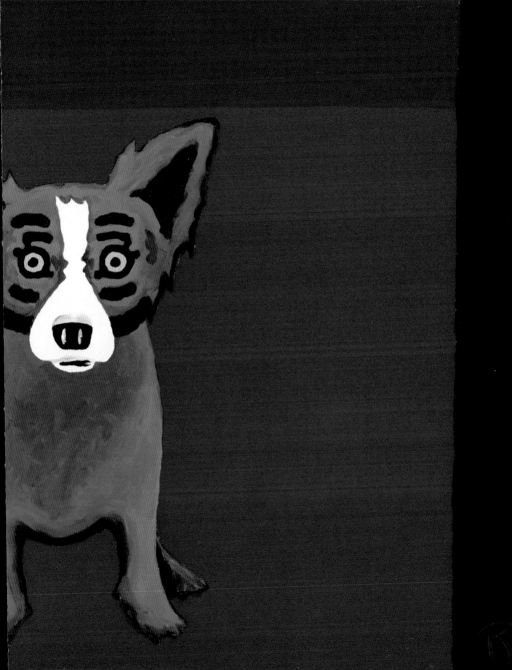

A Palette of Thought

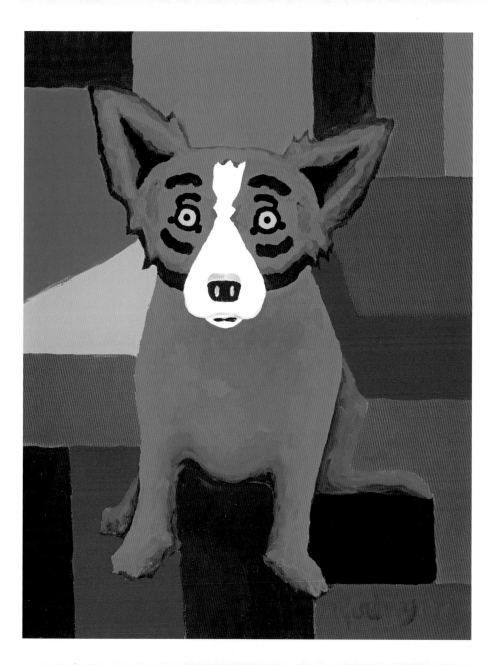

Blue

&

Little Blue

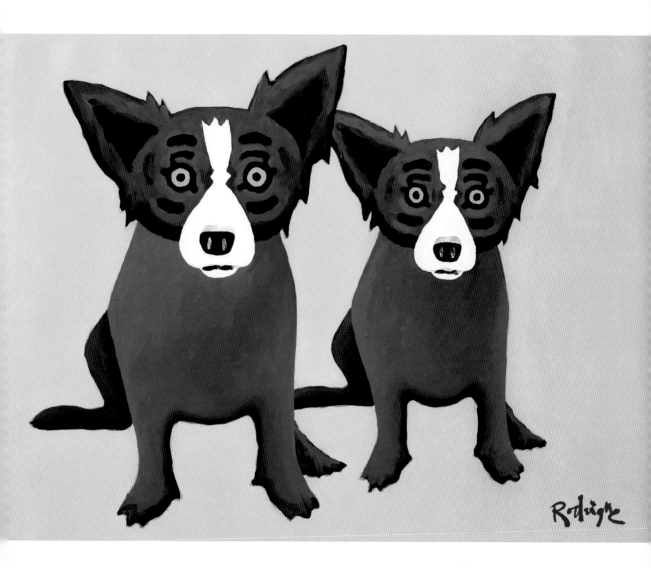

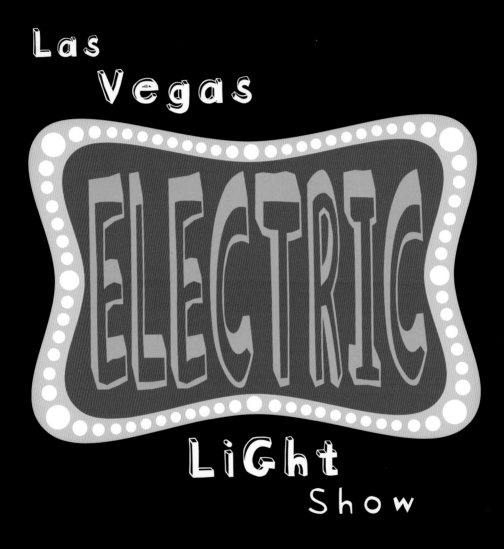

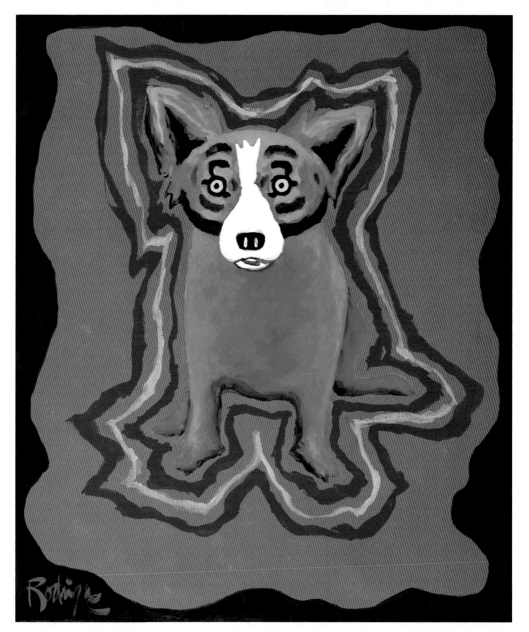

85

Born

with

a

GreEn

Thumb

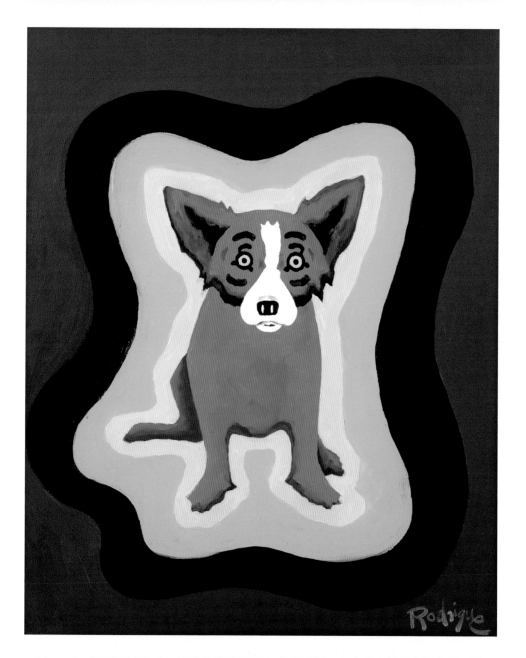

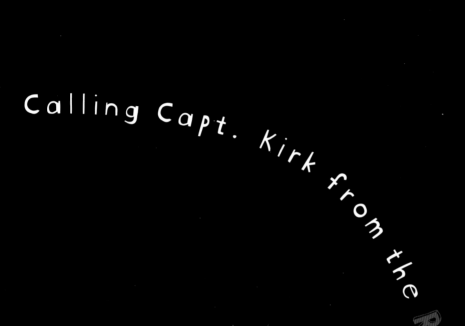

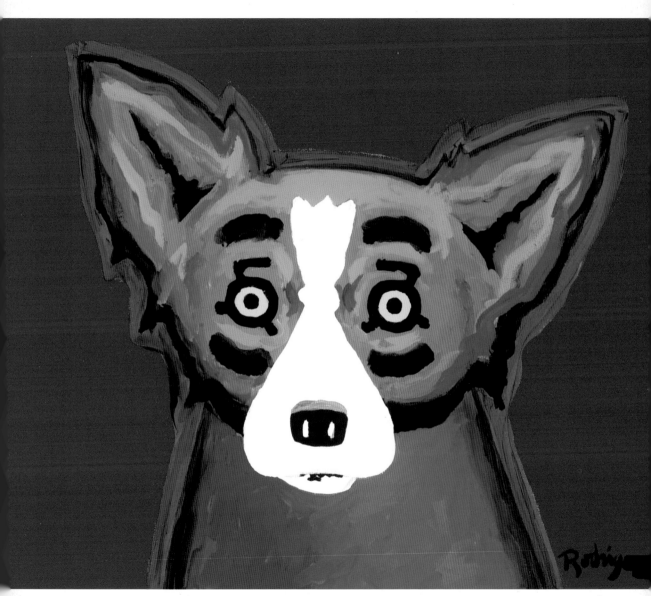

Blue

Pharoah

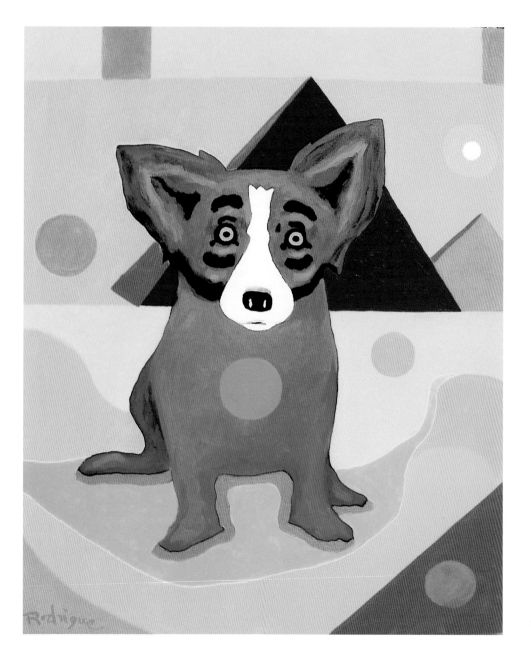

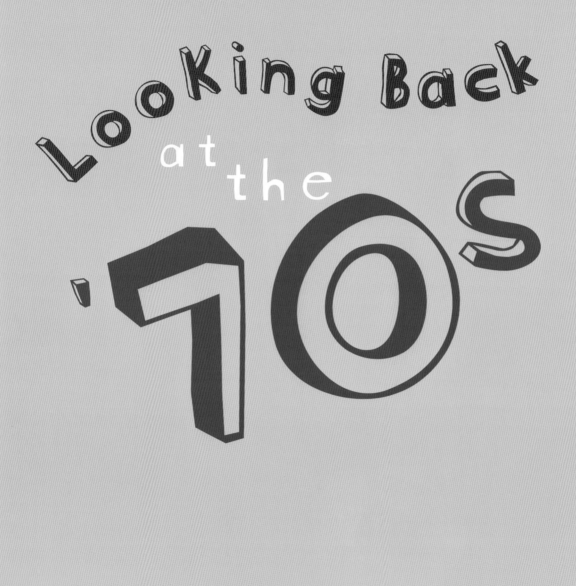

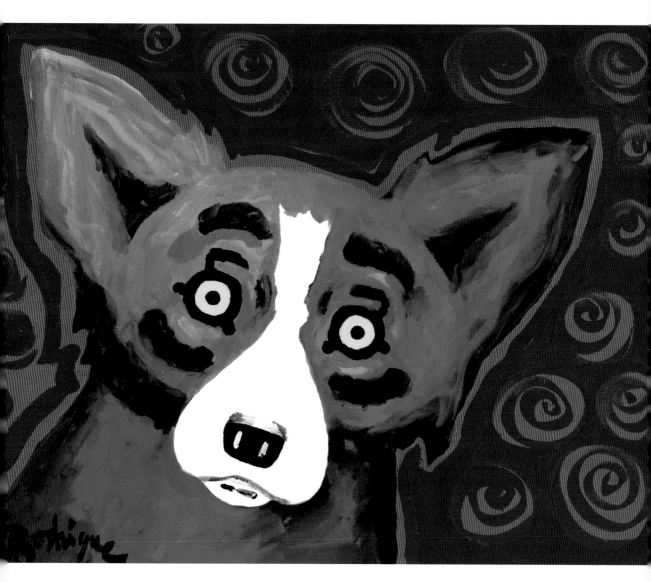

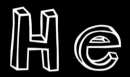

He

Answers

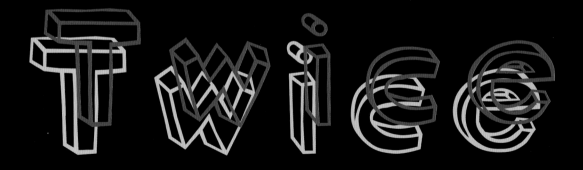

Twice

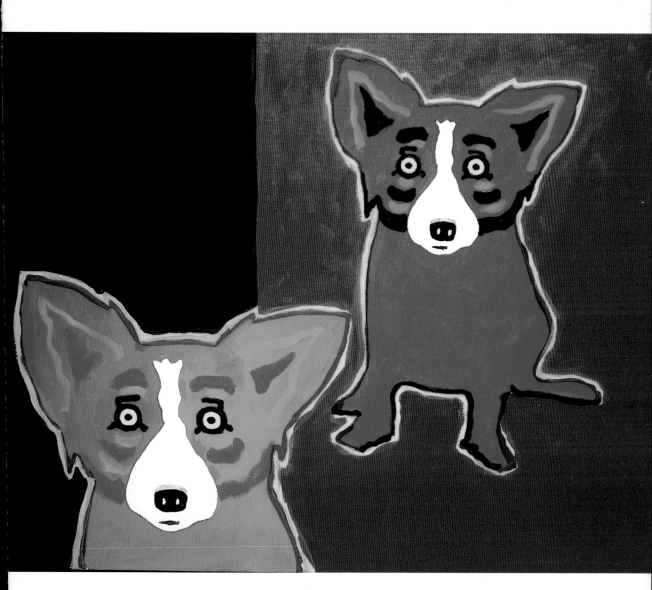

95

A Face iN tHe Crowd

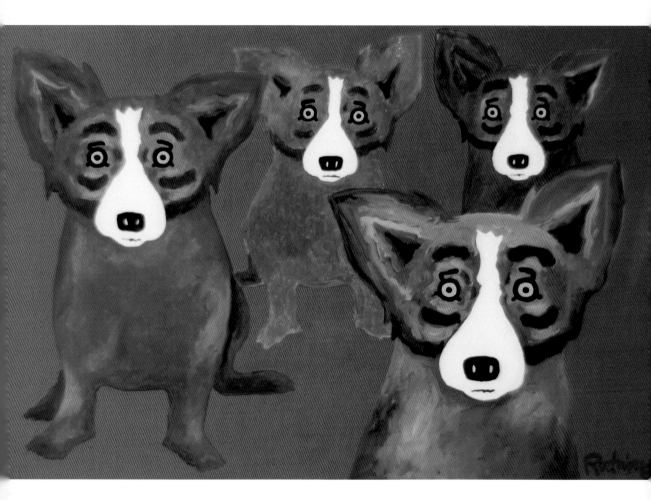

Mickey Mouse
Has
Nothing
on
Me

(Congo Dog)

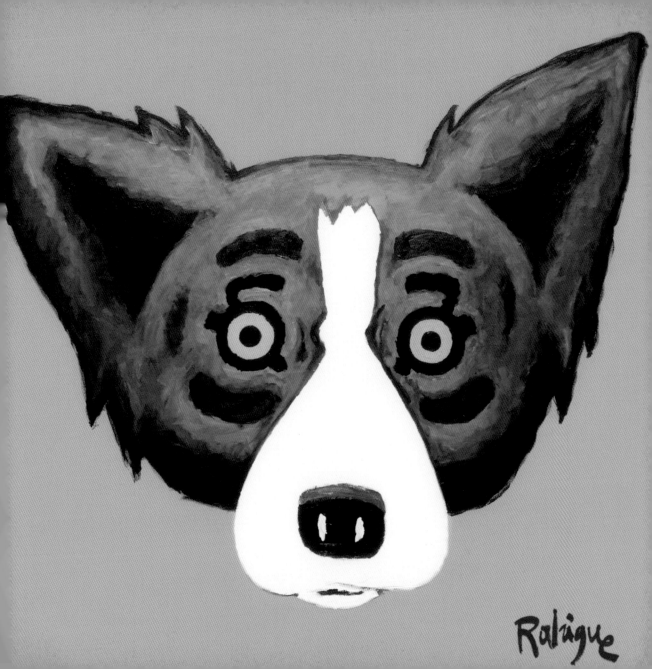
Rabague

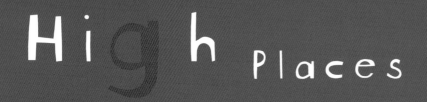

High Places

for Me

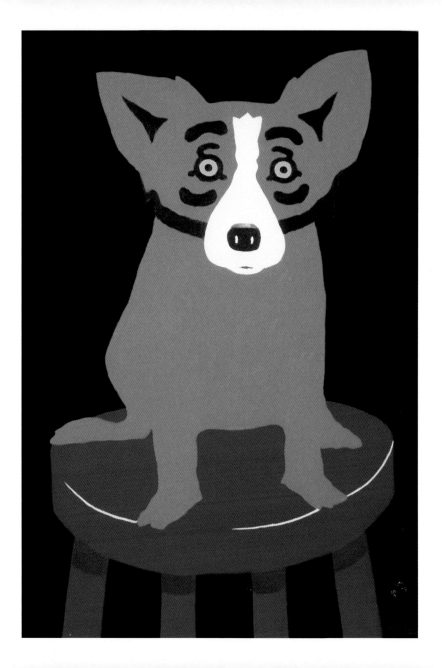

101

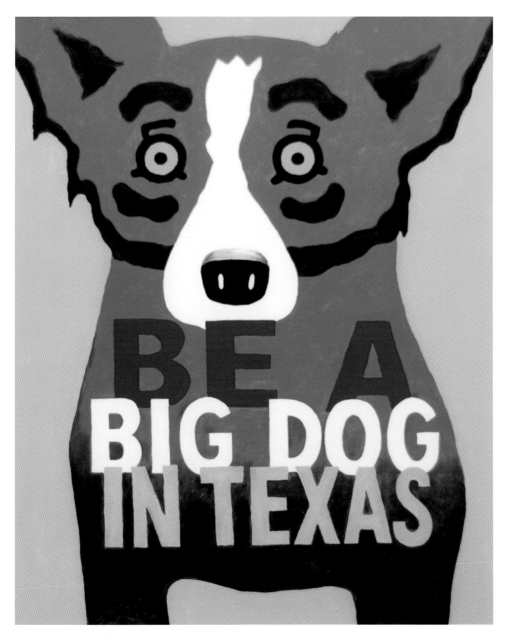

I'M SO Cool

I'M Hot

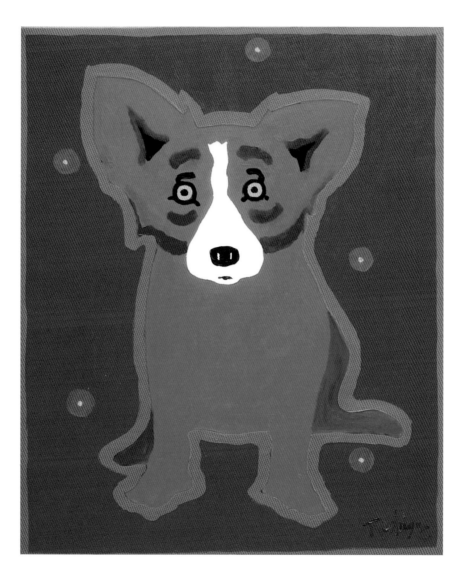

I've BeCome

a

Different

PerSon

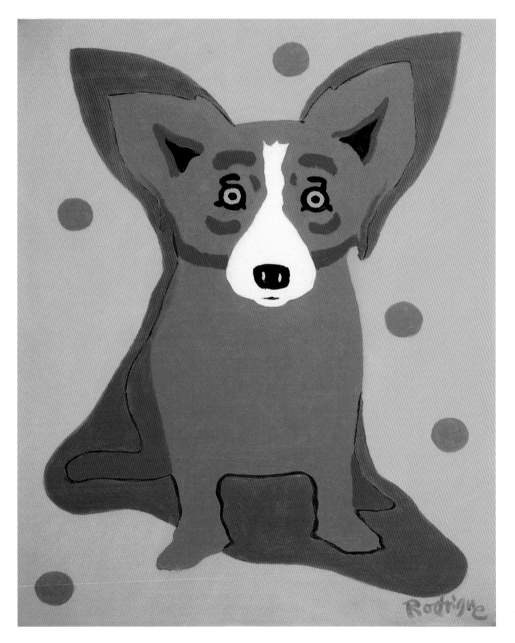

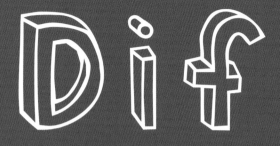

Dif
fer
ent

Opinions

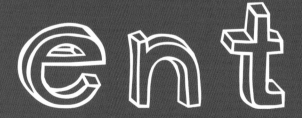

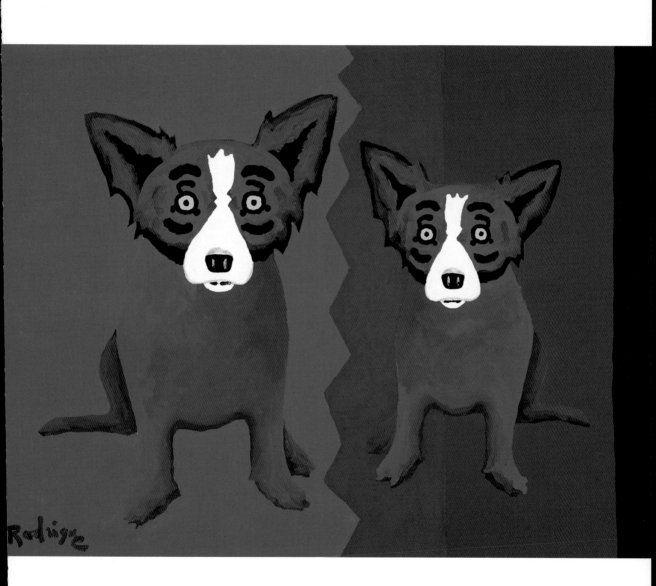

Ancestor

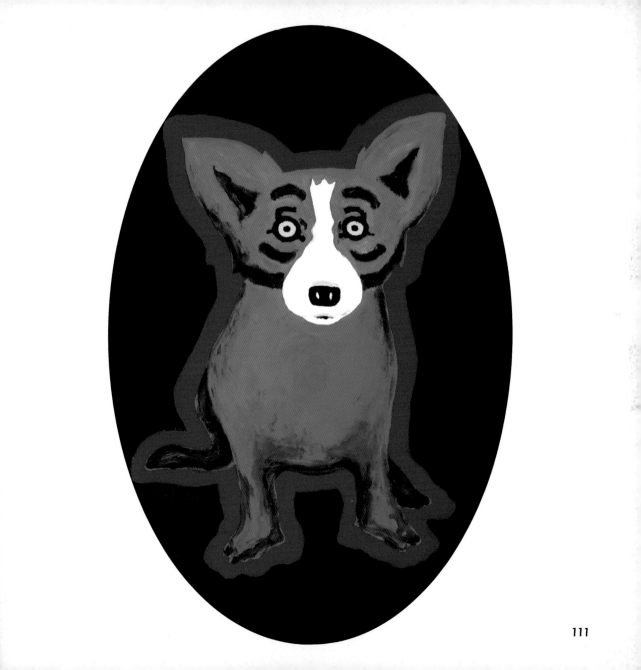

Jacques in a Box

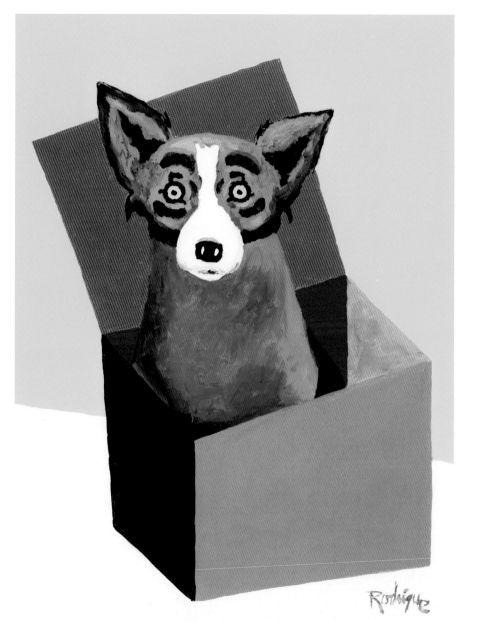

My Line

of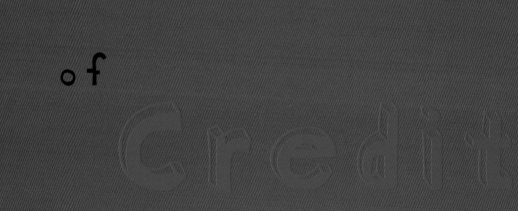

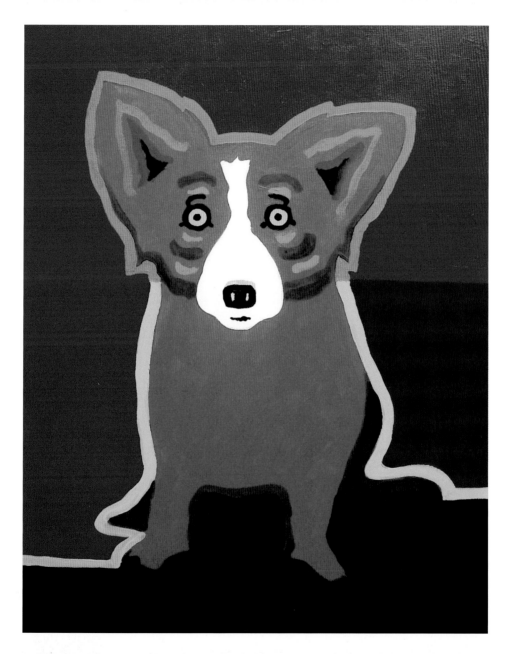

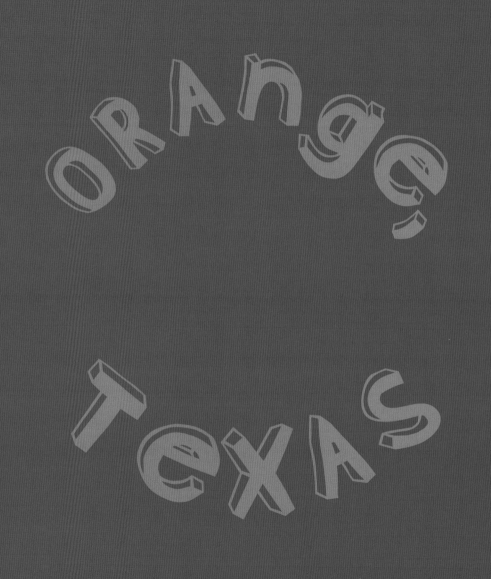

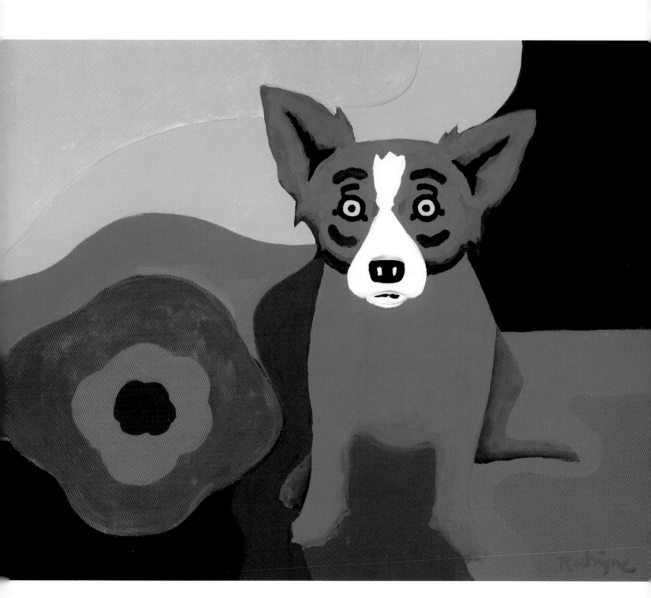

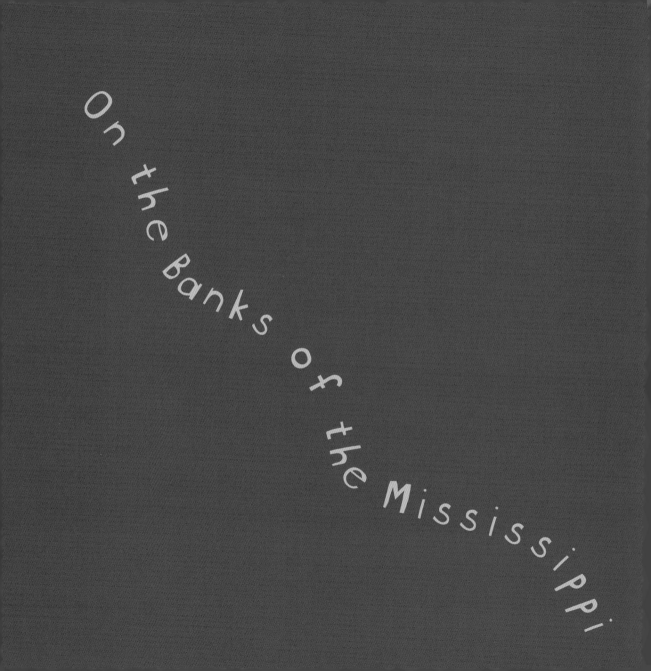

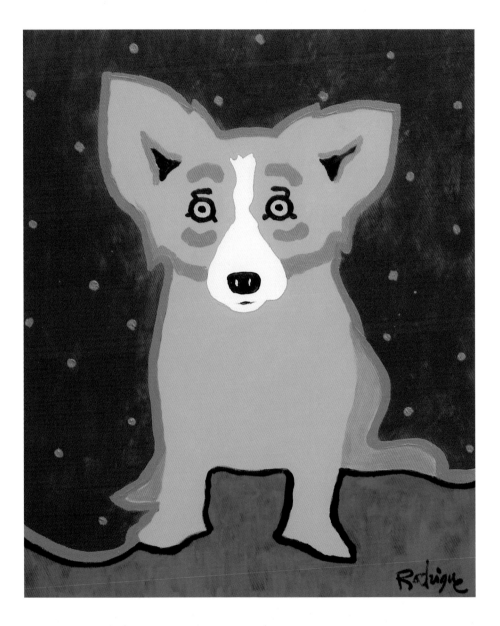

I See You
Forever

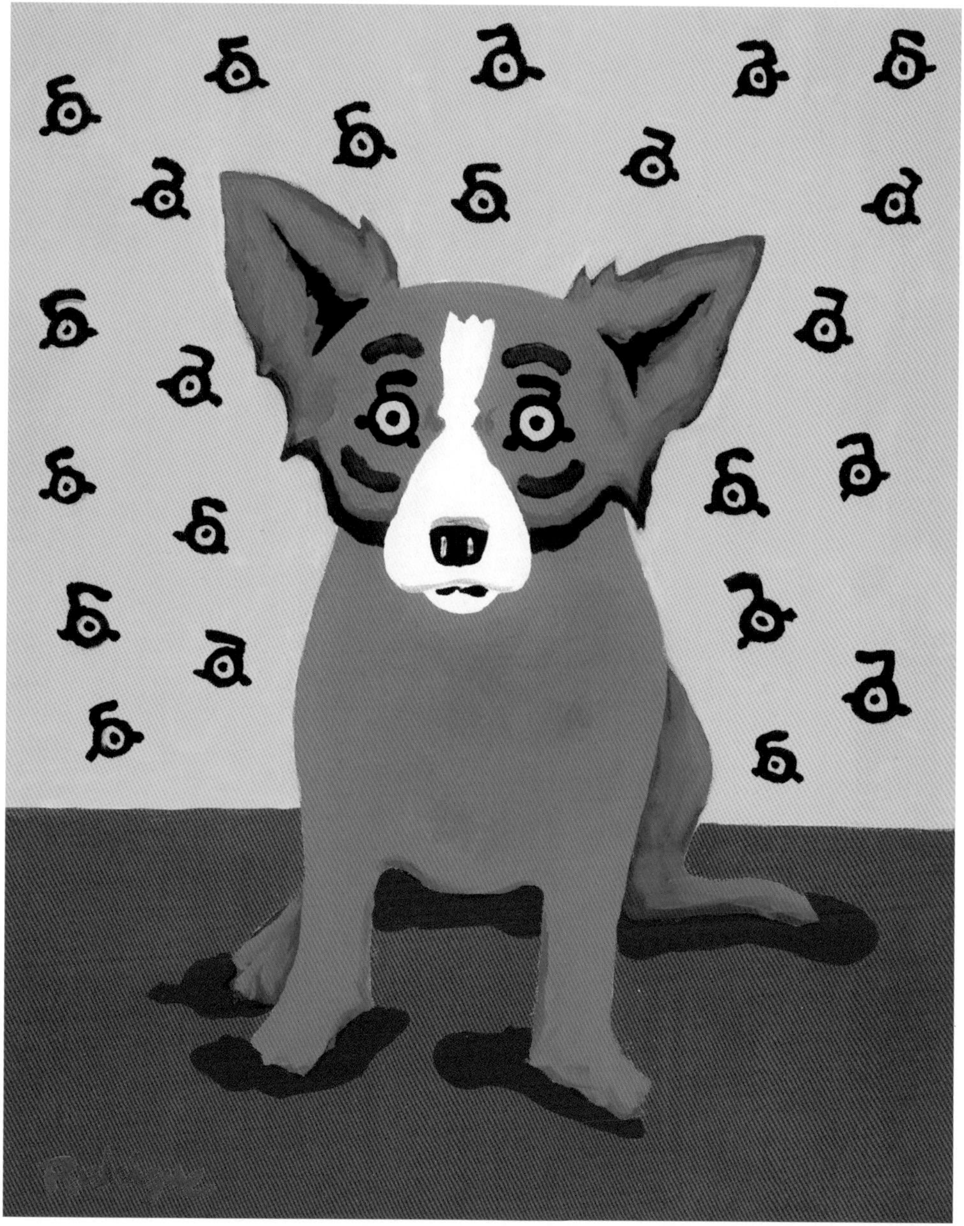

She's Startin' tO Stick oN me

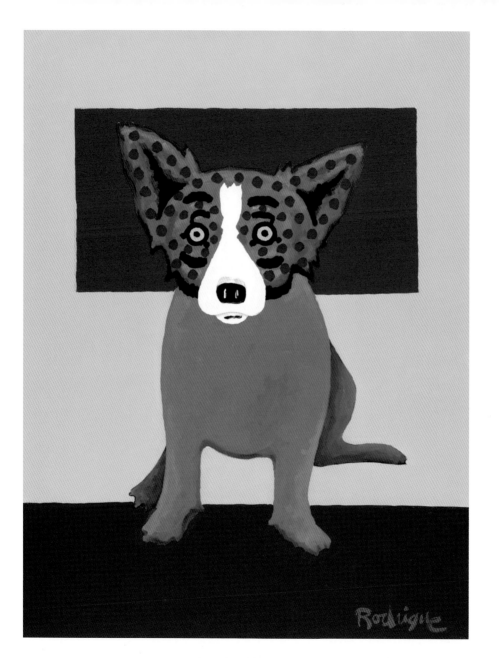

She

Called

ME   a

FrOg

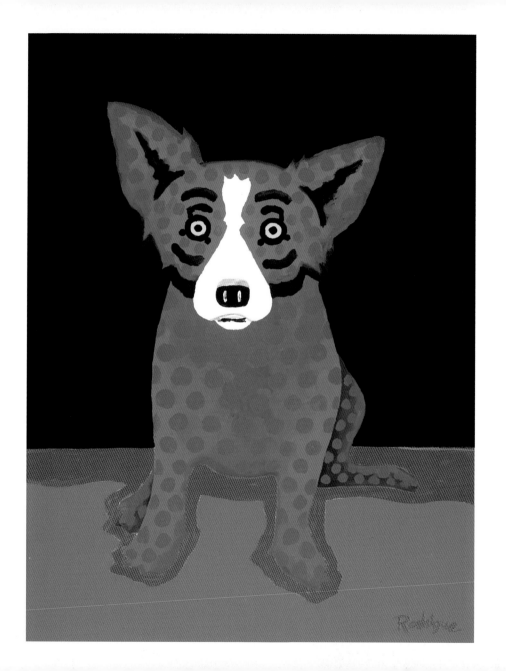

125

The BLUES

Make Me feel

Like an empty Box

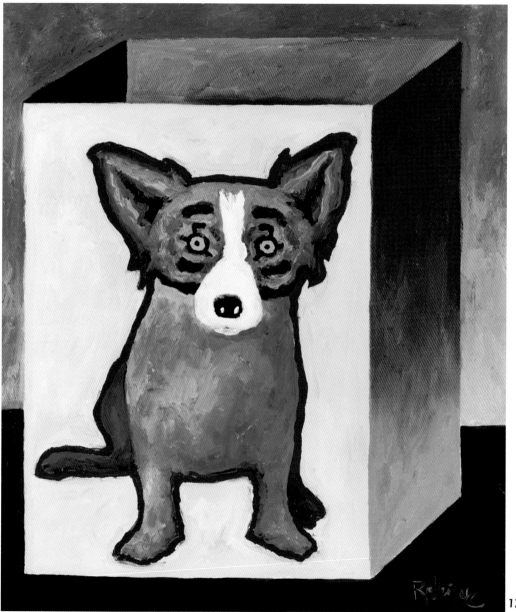

Box for a *for a* Cool Cat

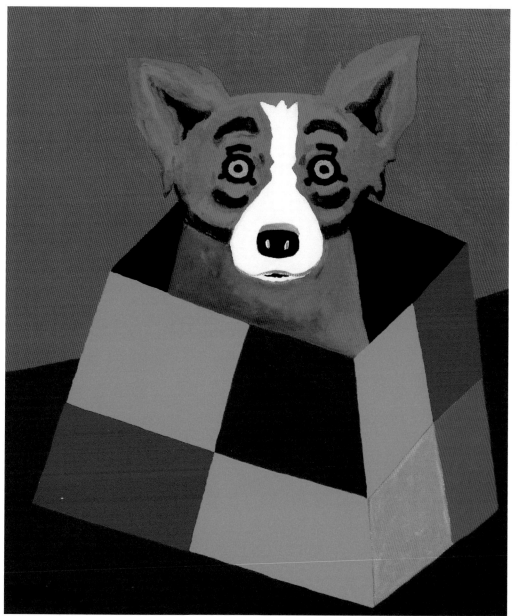

Reaching Out to New Friends

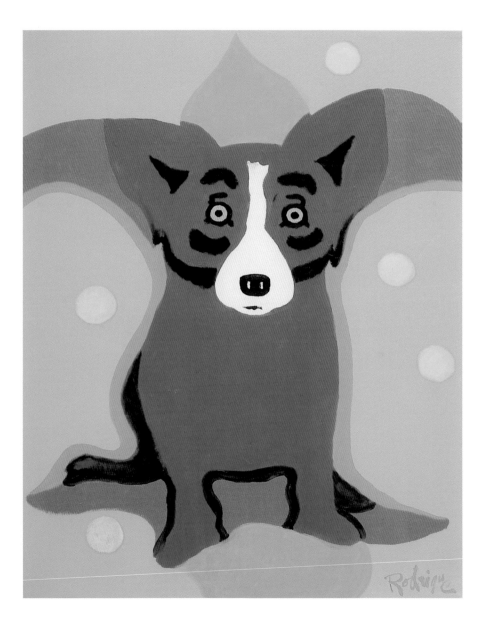

131

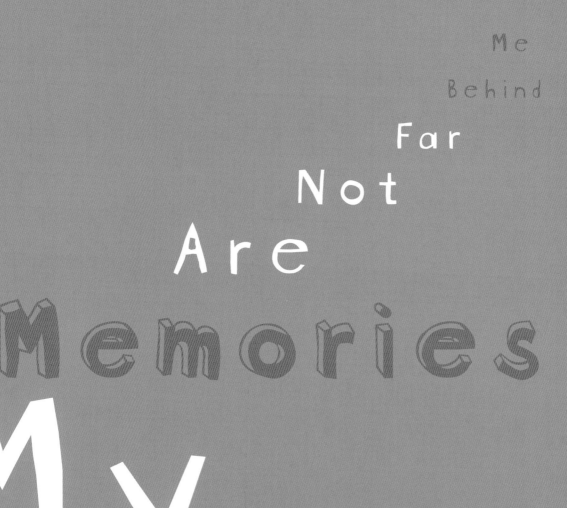

Me

Behind

Far

Not

Are

Memories

My

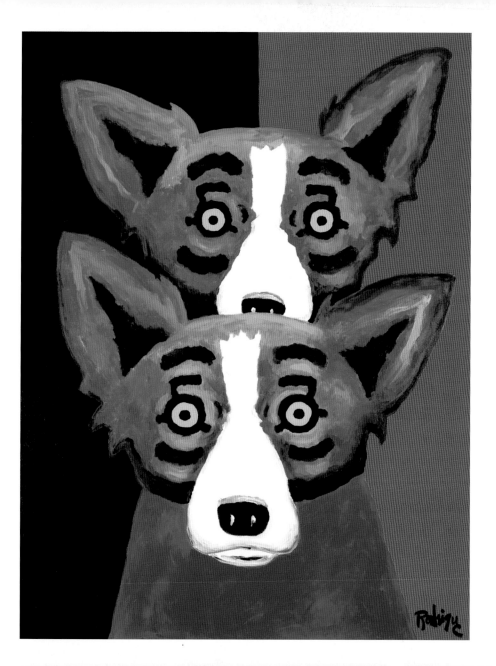

133

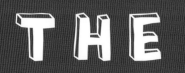

THE

DOG

WITHIN

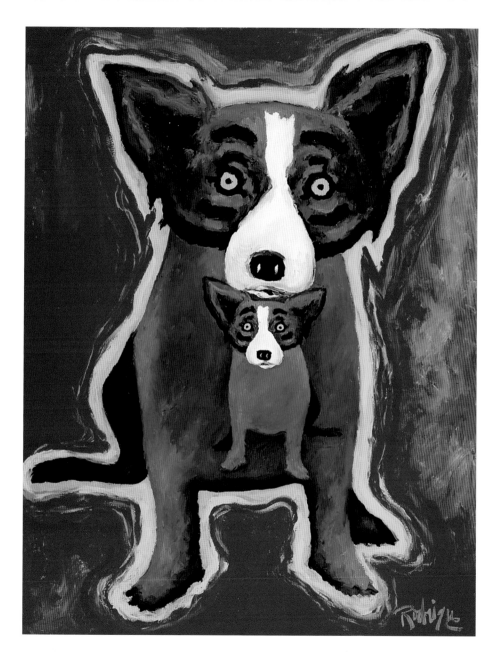

135

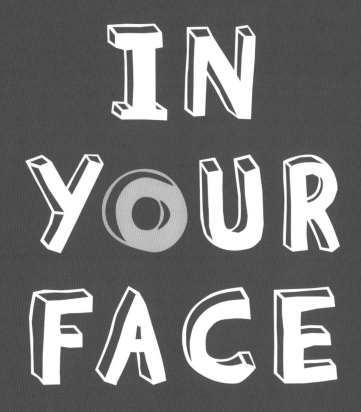

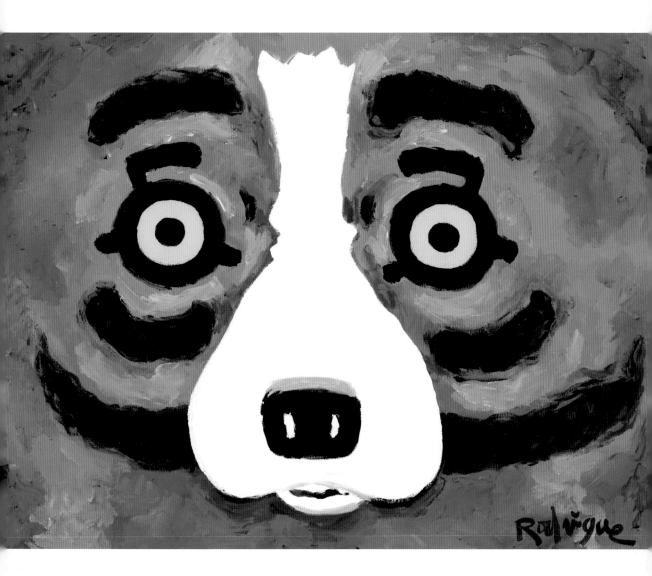

137

Everywhere
Everywhere
Everywhere
Everywhere
Everywhere
Everywhere
Everywhere
Everywhere
Everywhere

Everywhere

Everywhere
Everywhere
Everywhere
Everywhere
Everywhere

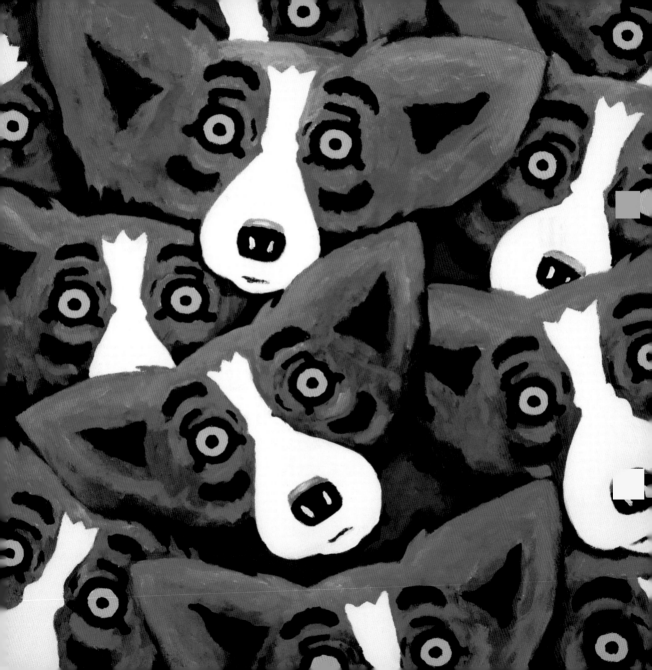

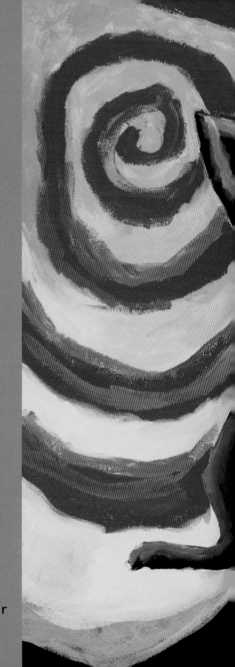

4

Spiraling out

We Are Spirits Together

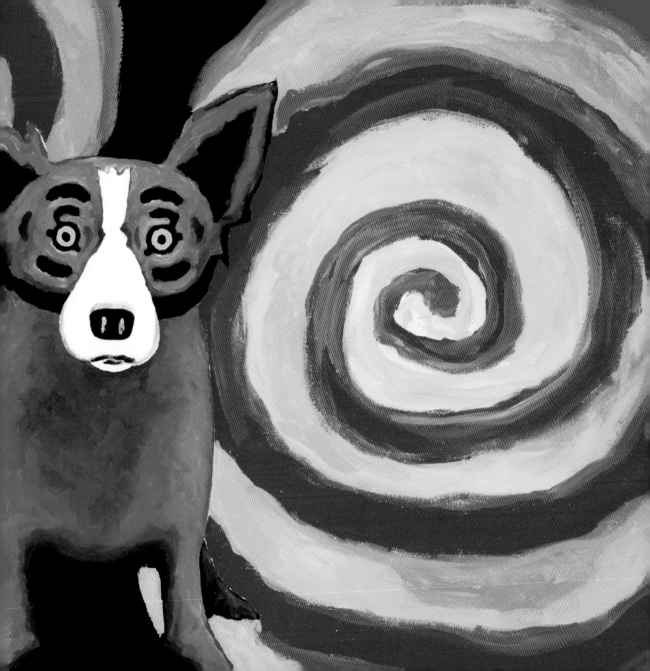

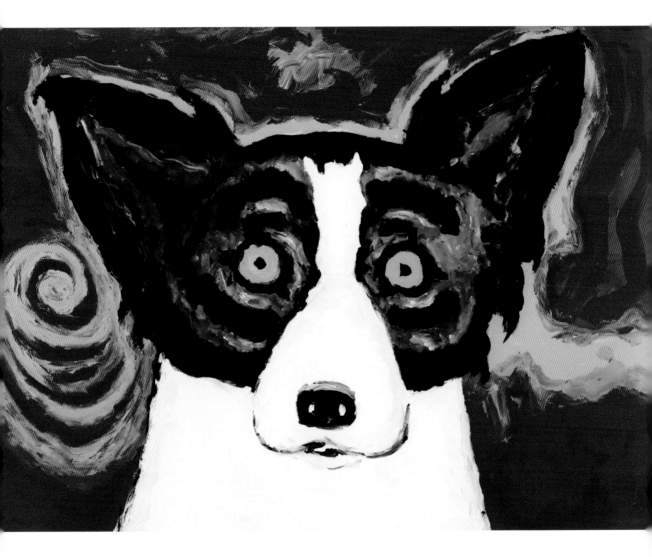

Mr. Watson, Come Here .

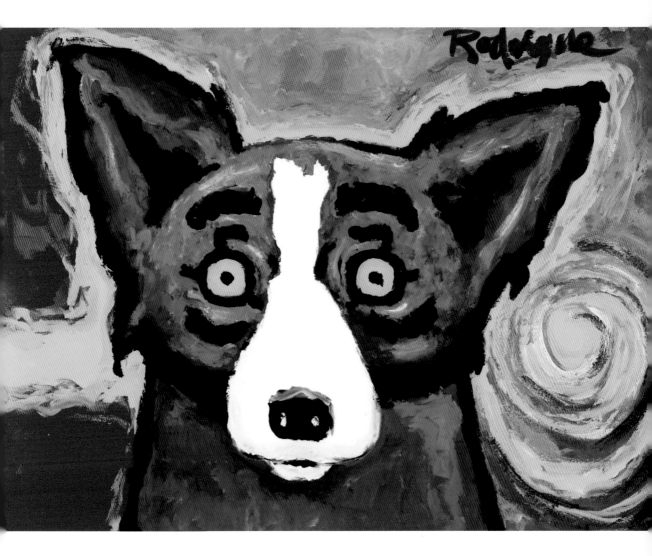

. . I NEED YOU

143

Hurricane Romance

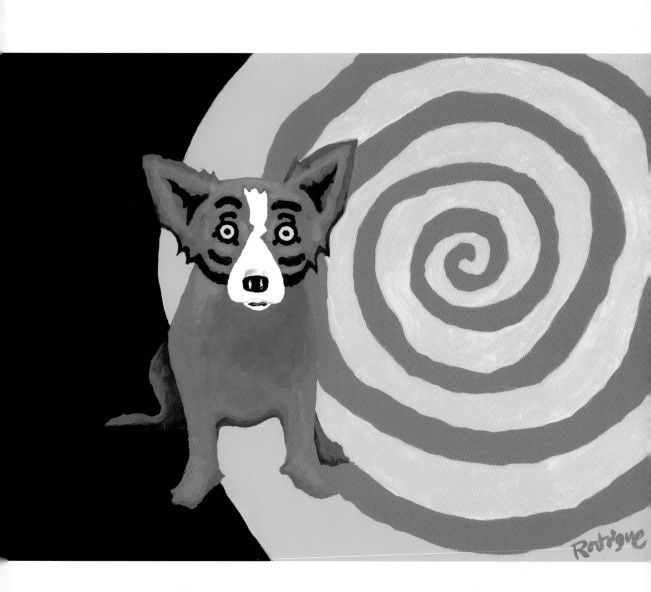

Eye of the

Hurricane

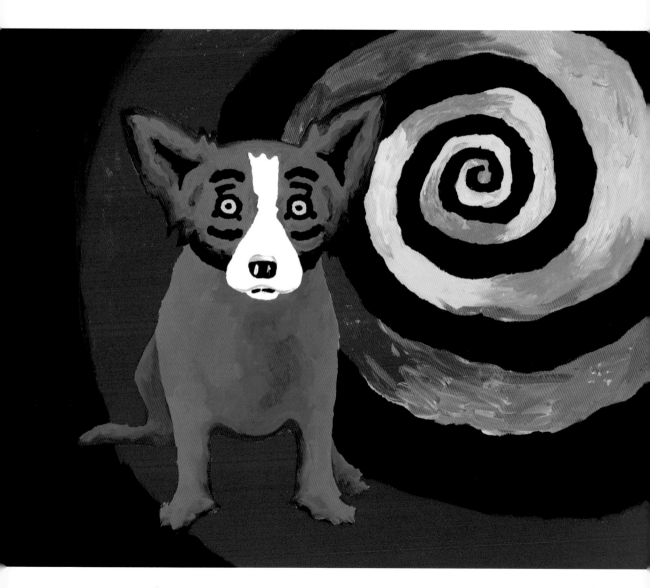

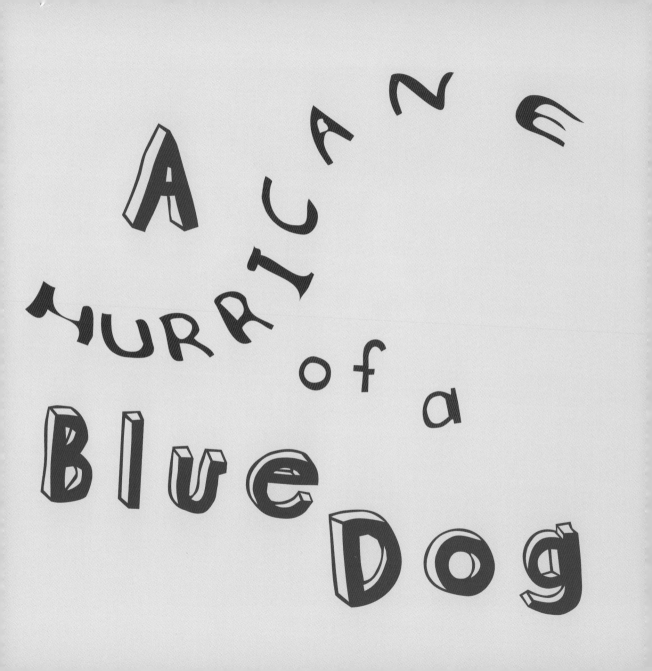

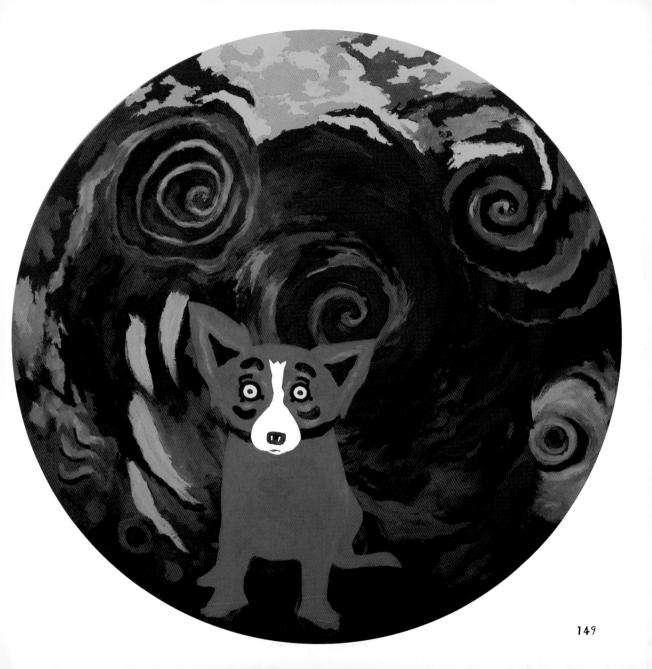

149

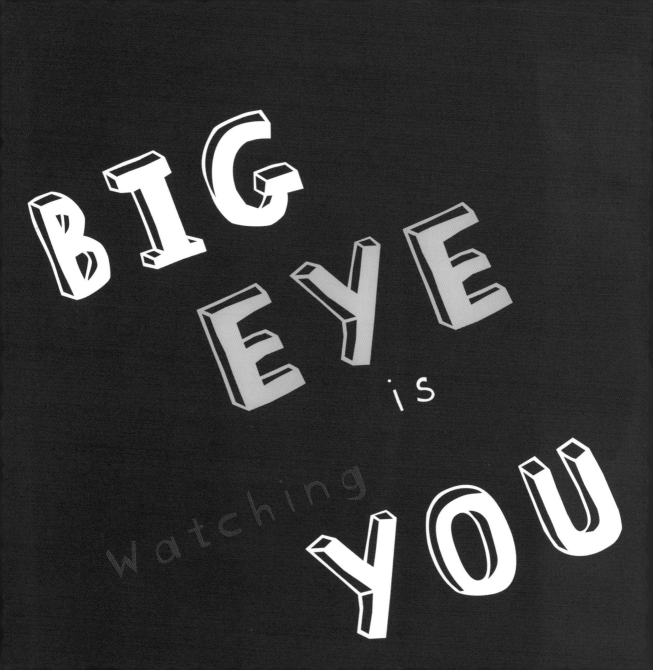

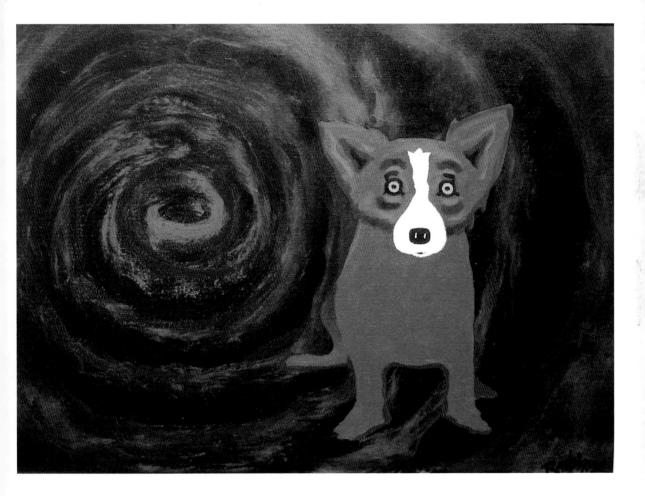

151

The Summer of '06

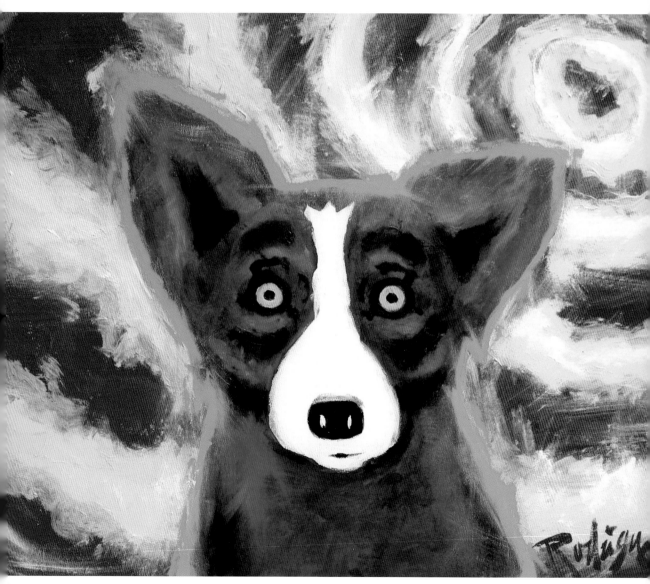

153

Crossroads of my Life

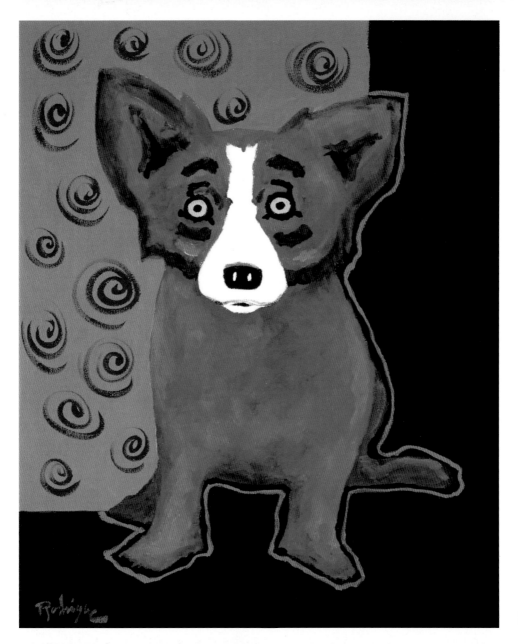

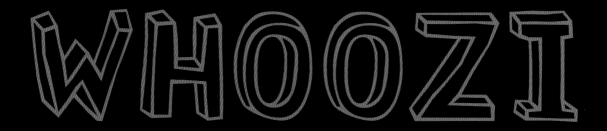

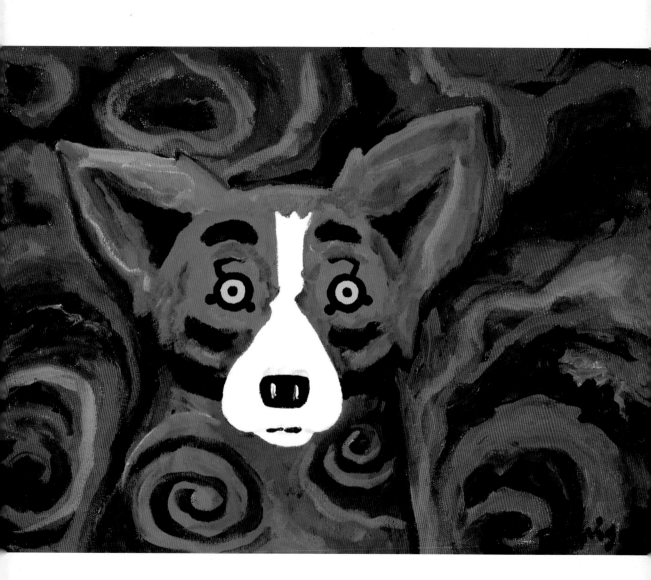

It Was a

BaD

Night

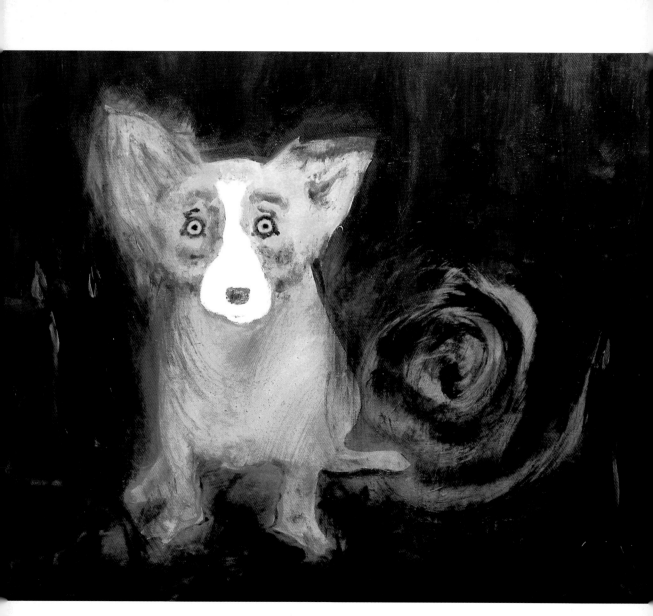

I've Got to Straighten Out My Life

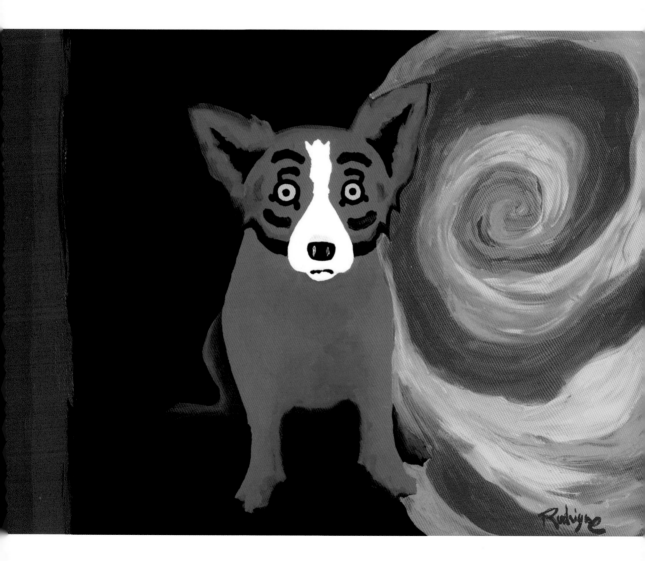

LOVE
Brings
Out
the
Sunshine

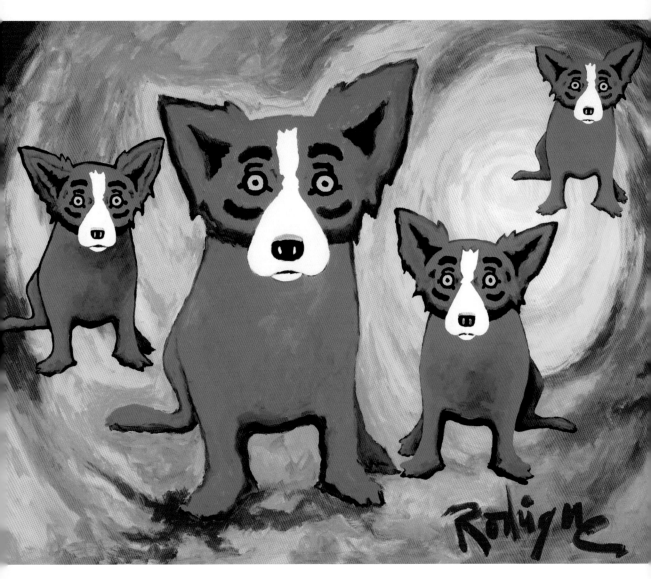

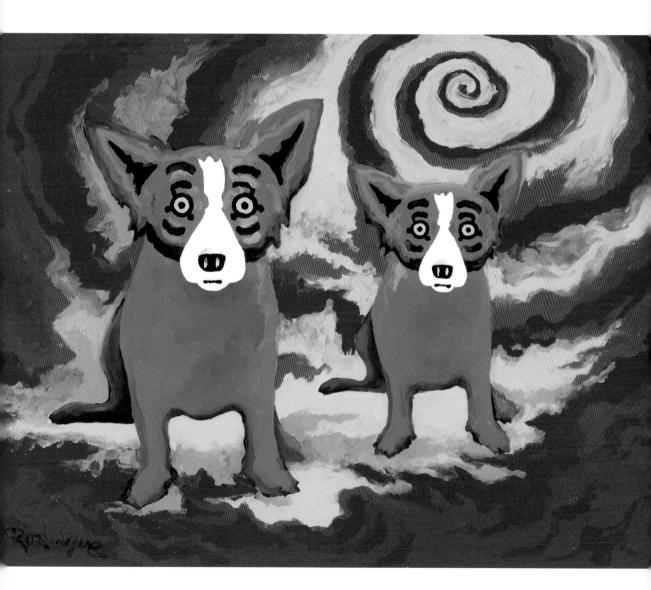

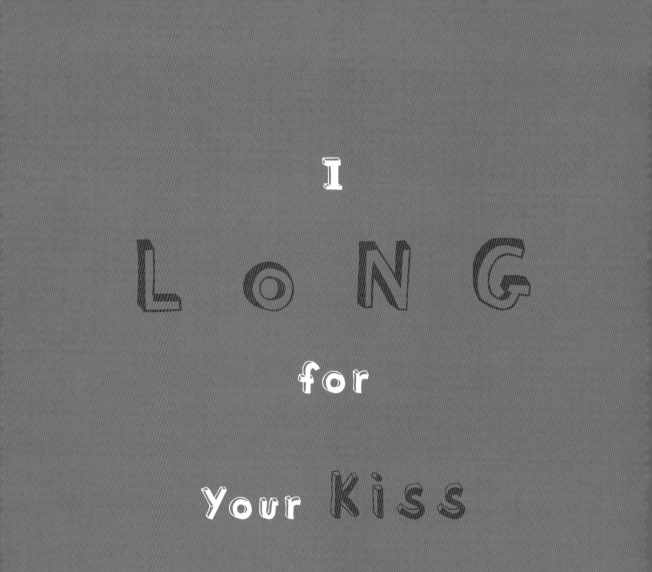

I

LoNG

for

Your Kiss

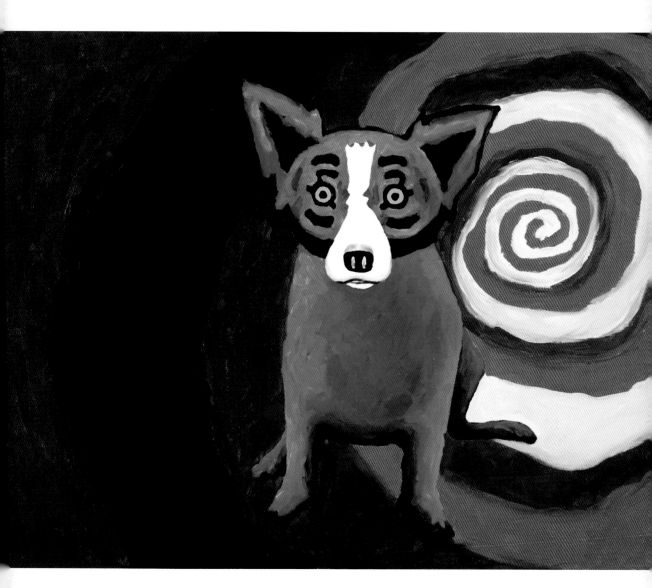

Light
My
Fire
Tonight

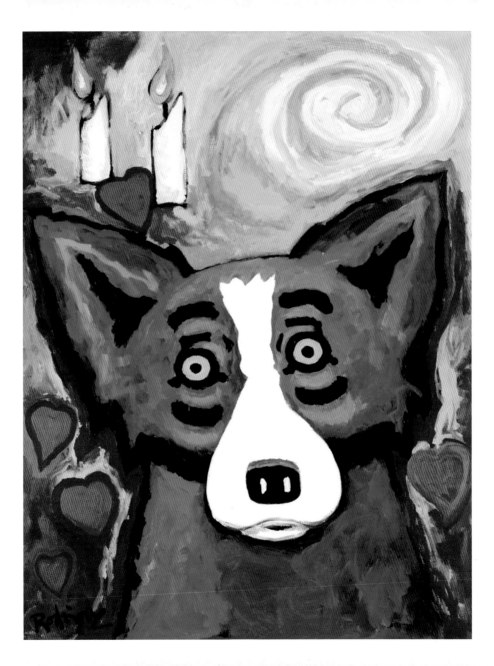

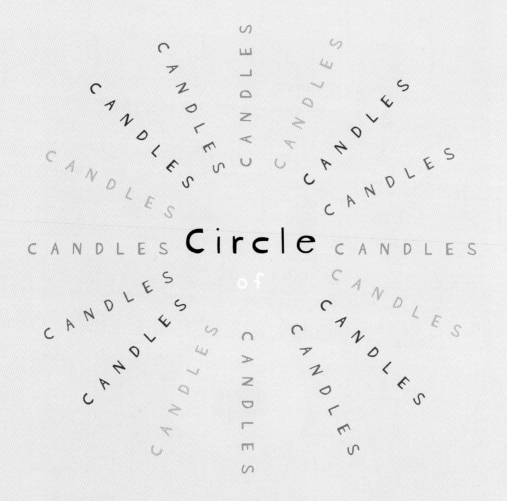

Circle of Candles

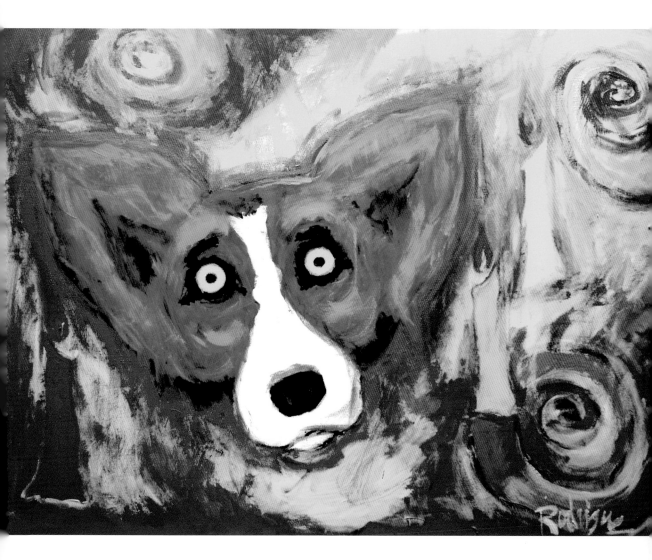

Candles

in tHe

Wind

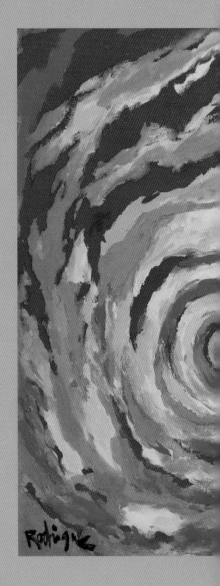

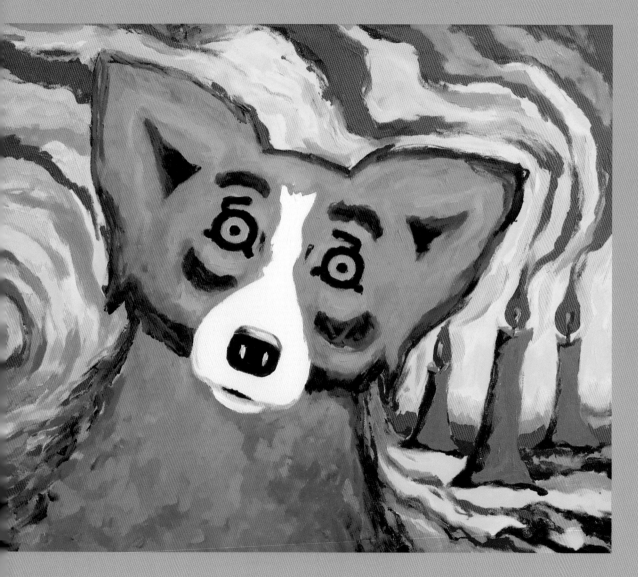

5
The
Art
of
ExpreSsion

Underneath a Warm Blanket of Love

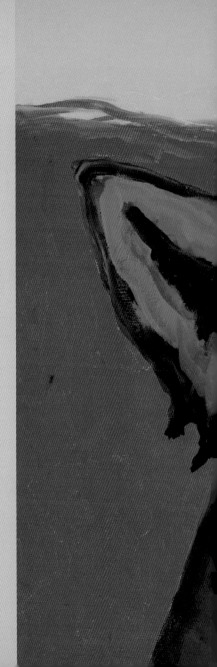

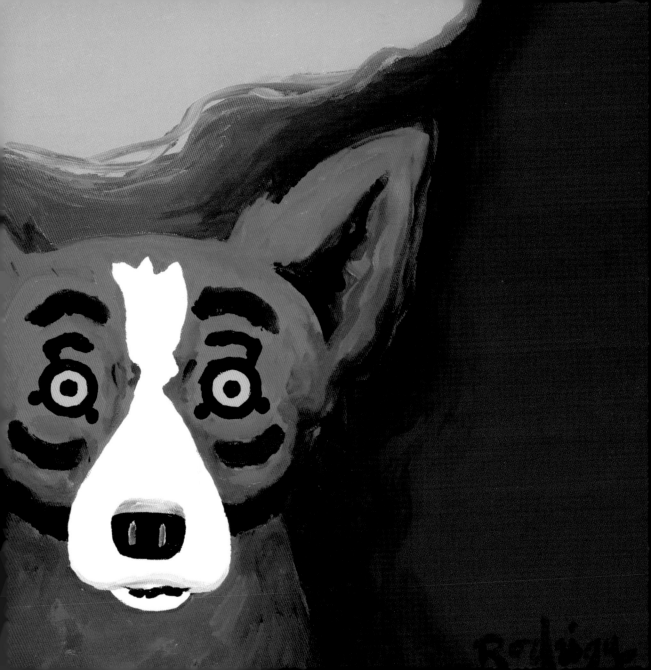

I Am an Artist

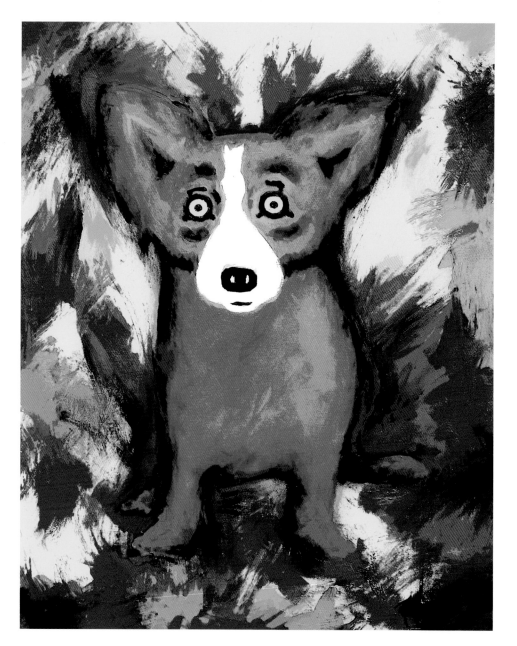

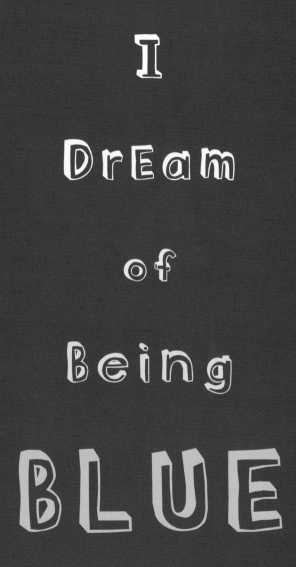

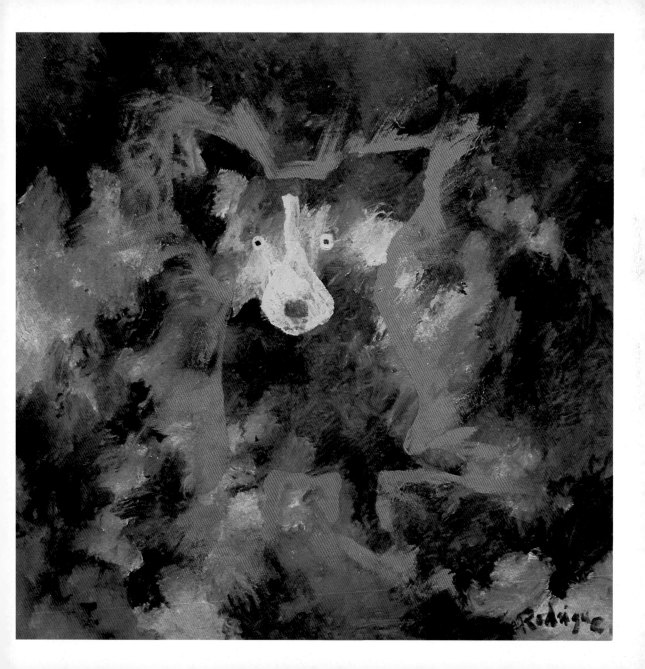

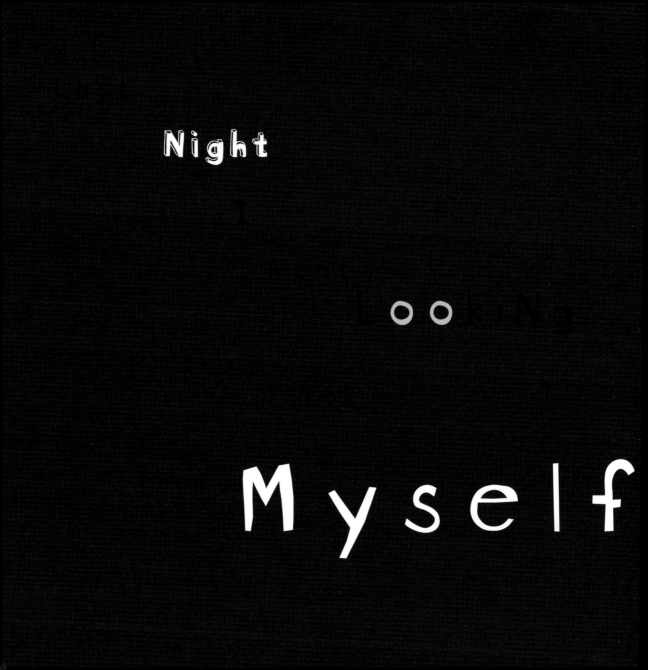

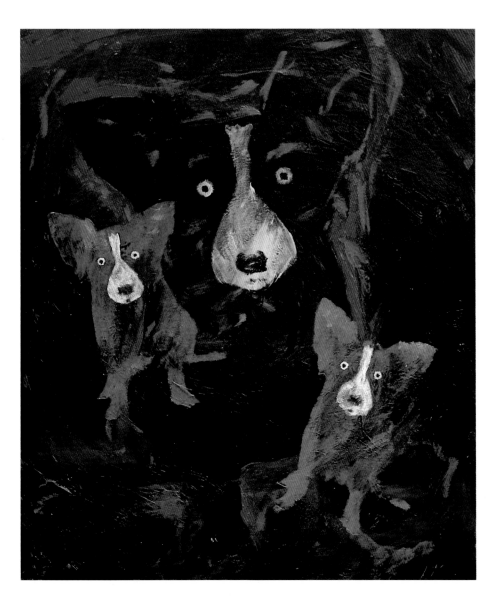

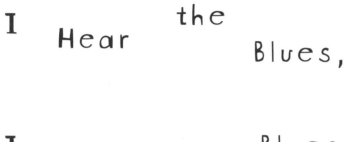

I Hear the Blues,

I See the Blues,

I Sing the Blues

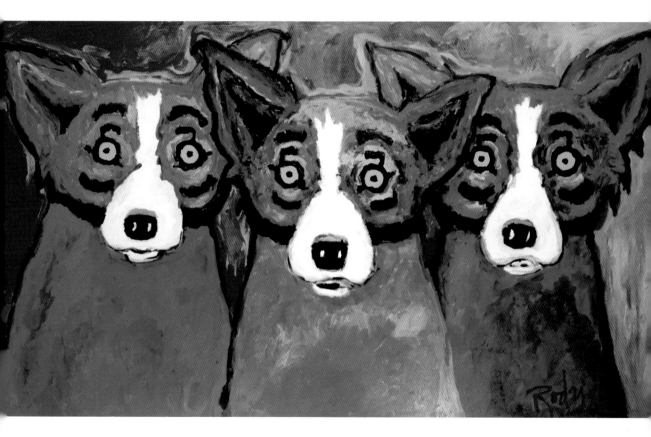

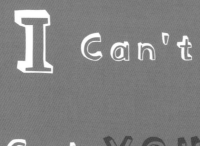

I Can't

Get YOU

Off My

mind

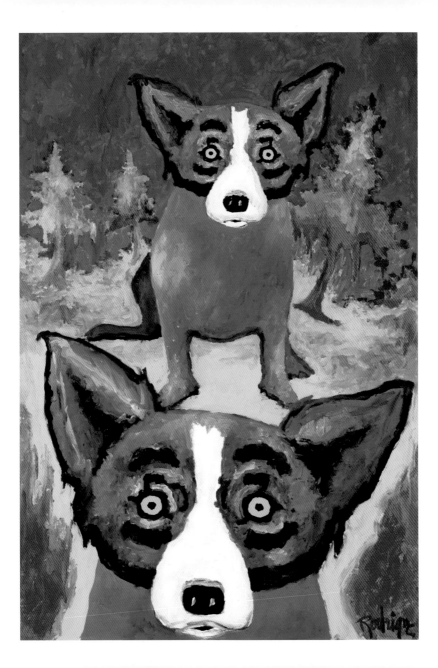

185

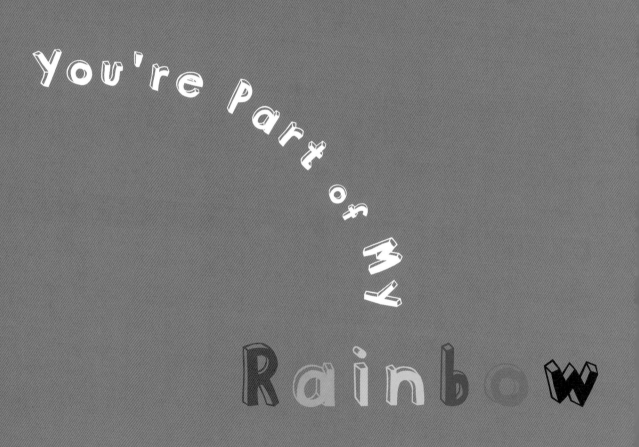

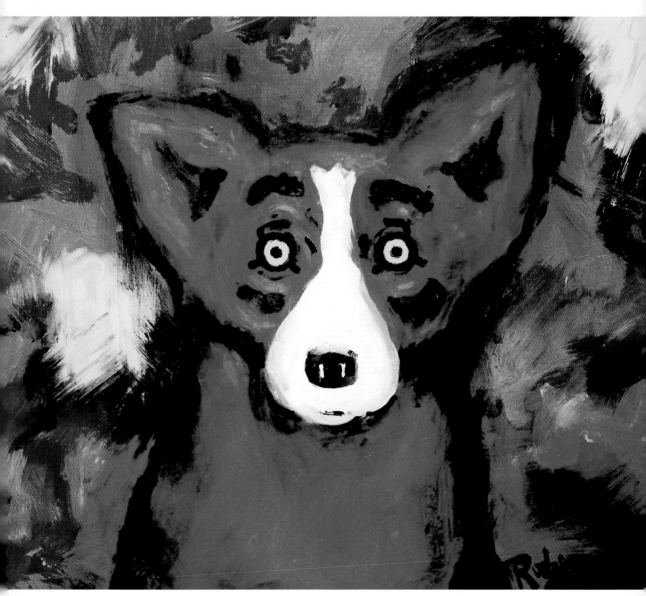

HeaRts

in

LoVE

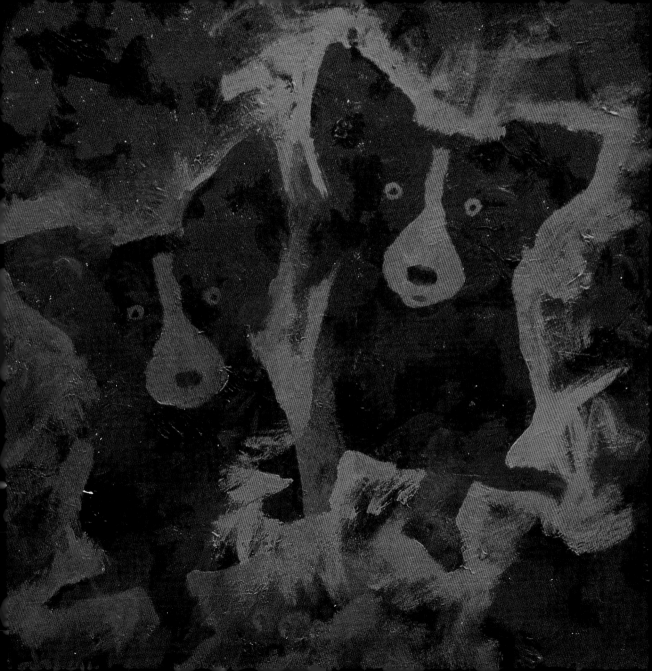

You're the Only One Under the Sun

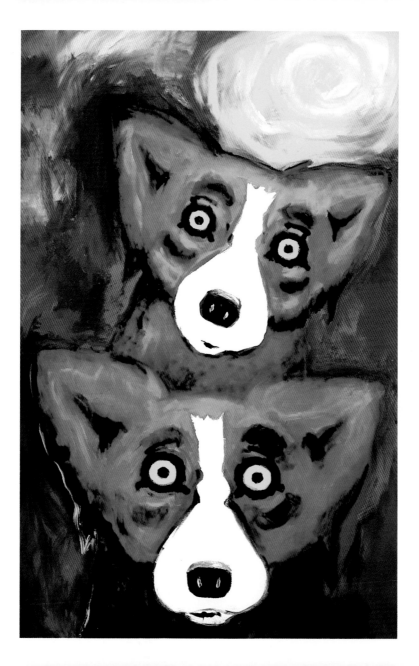

Half

of

Me

Loves

You

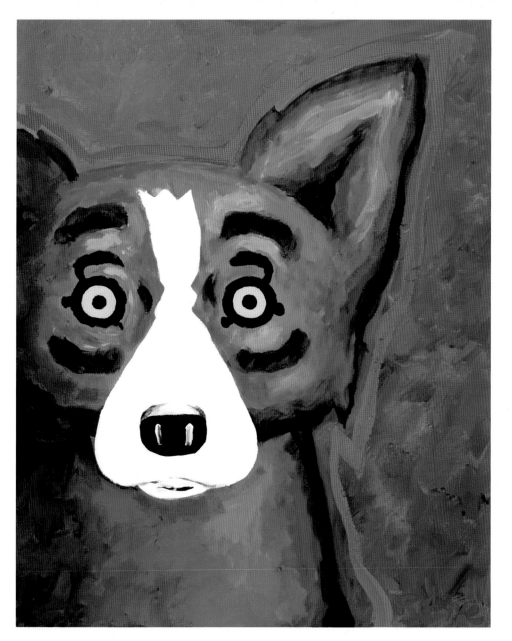

I've Been Known to

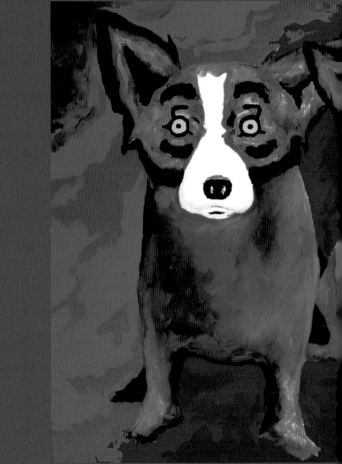

Change My Position

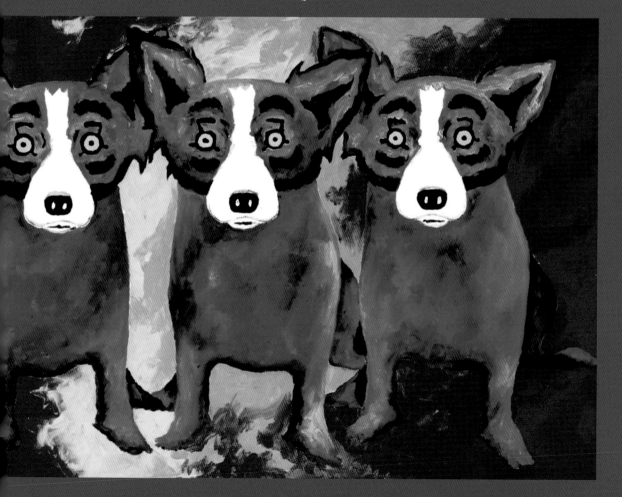

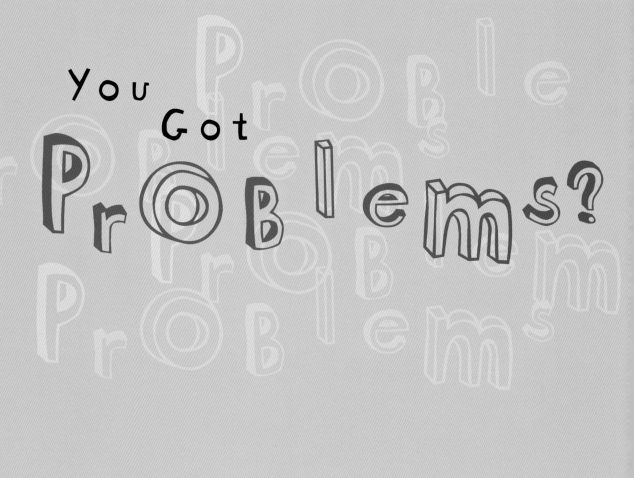

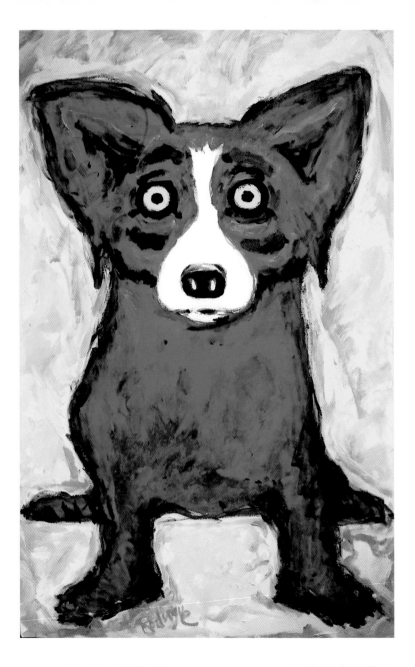

197

In

the

Greenhouse

Again

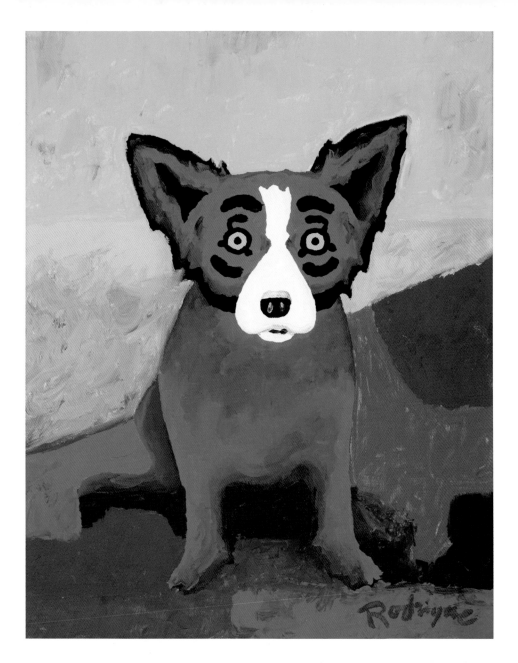

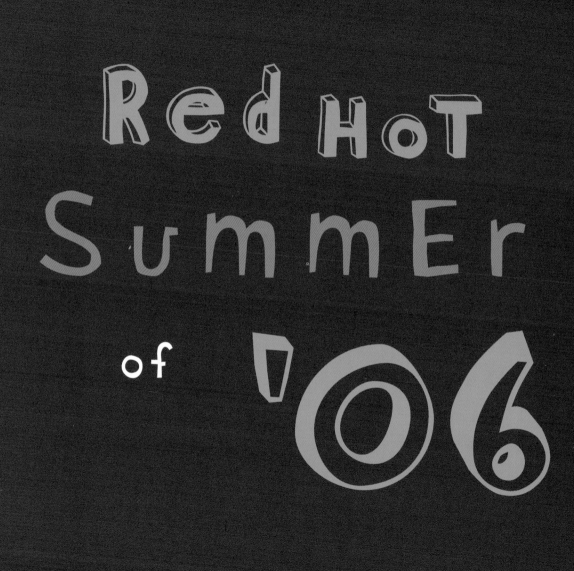

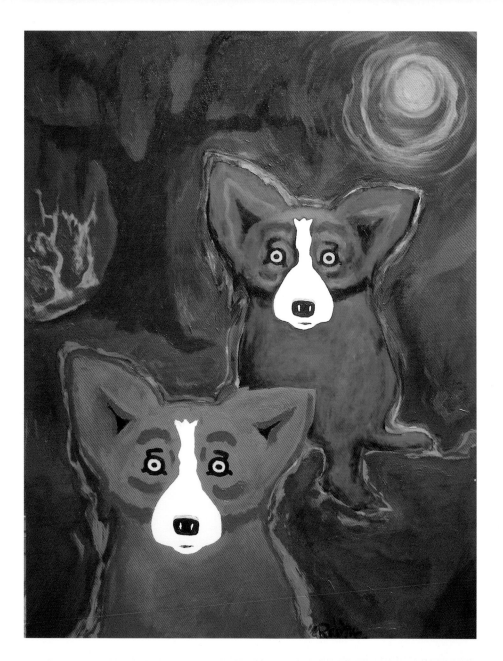

A

Mardi
Gras

Night

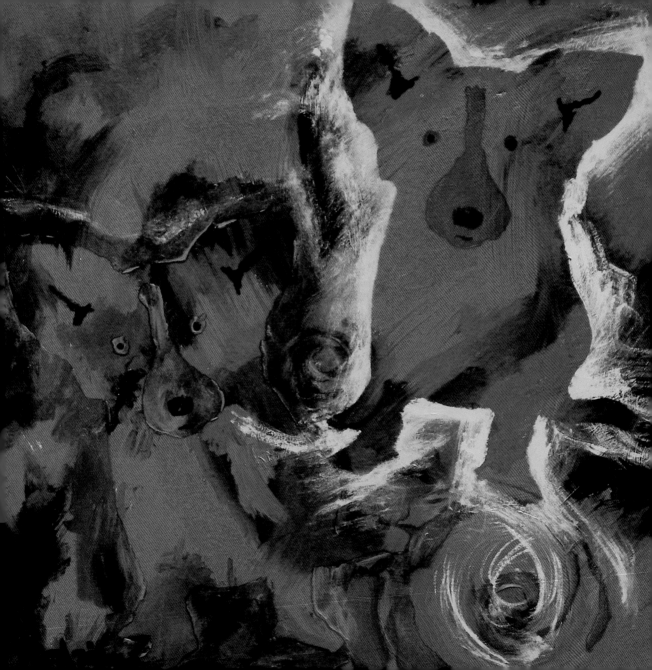

BLACK

MAGIC

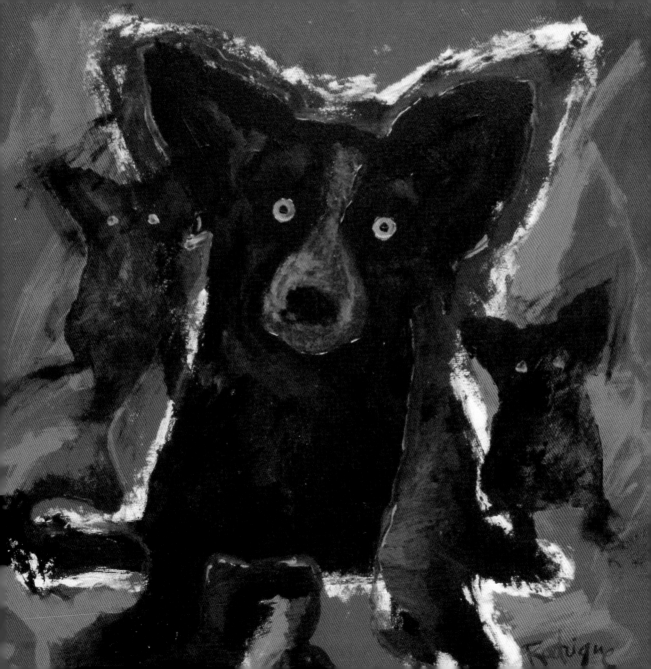

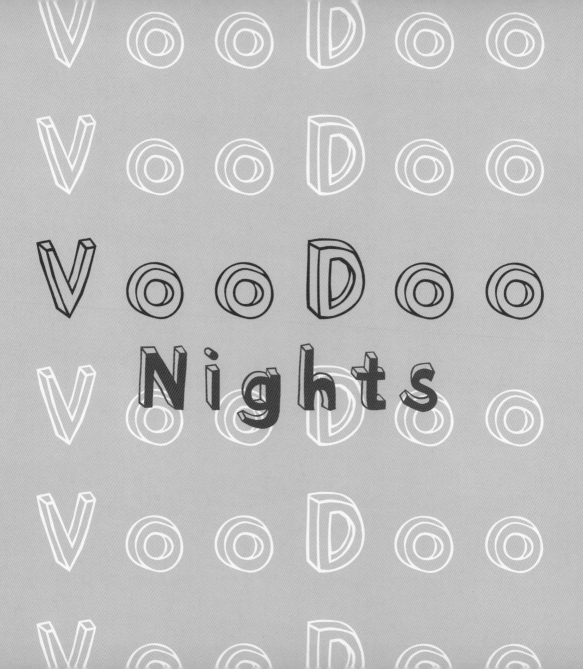

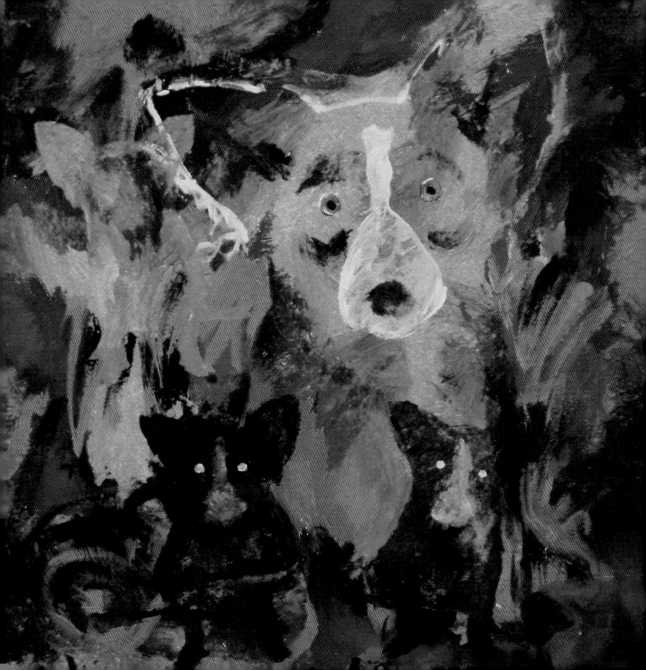

Midnight

Life

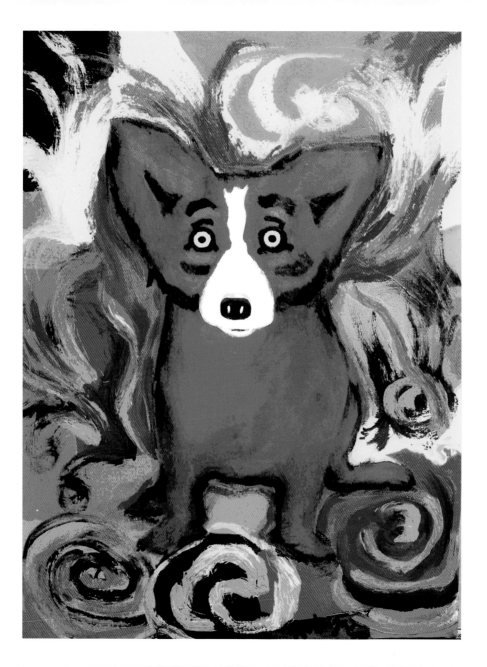

209

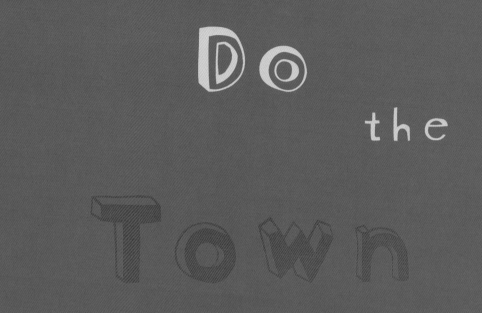

Do the Town Tonight

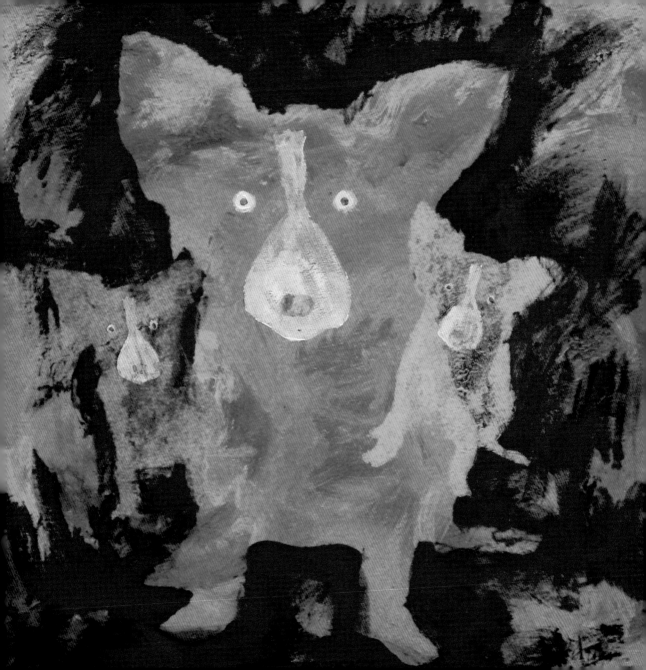

Blue

Dog

on

the

River

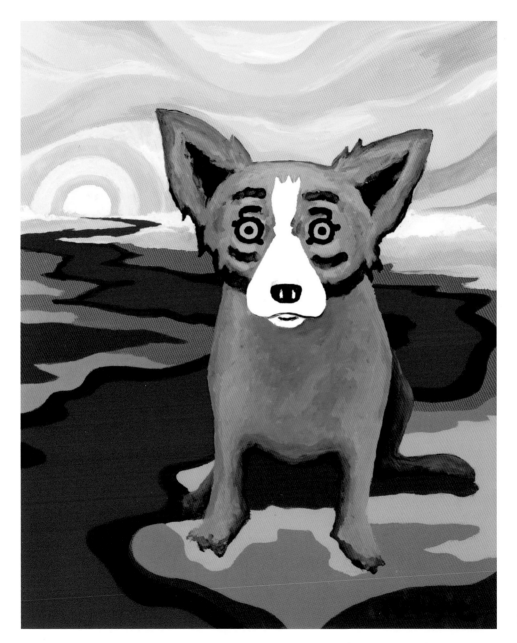

It's Been

a

Hot Cold

Night

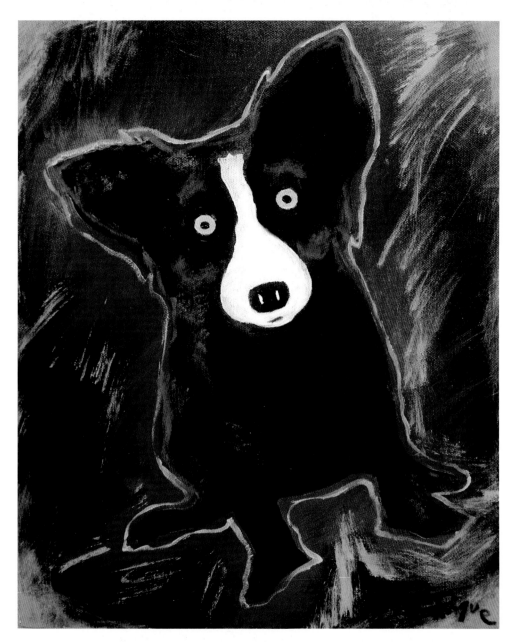

215

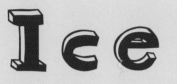

Ice

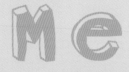

Me

Down

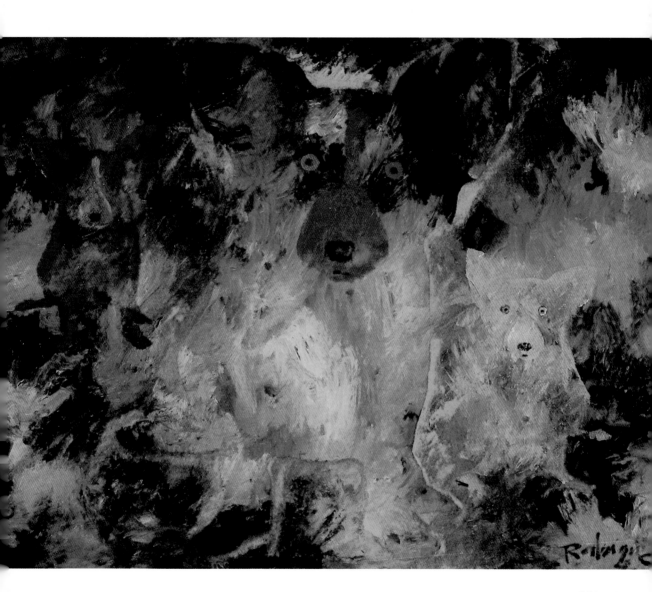

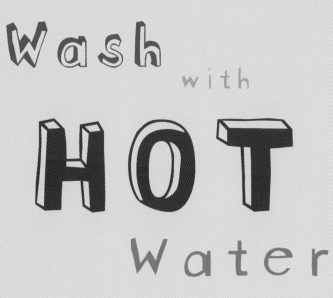

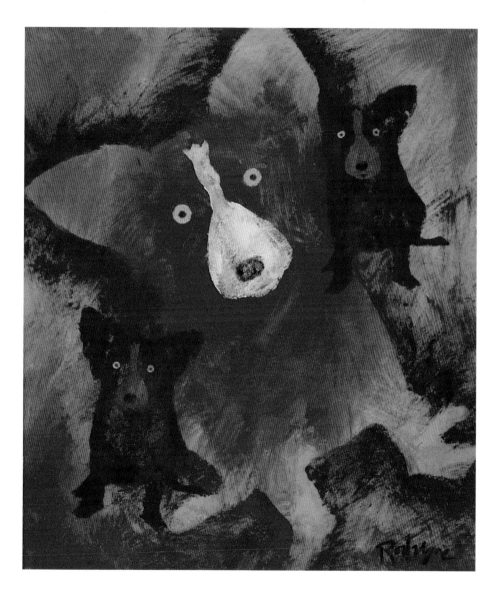

219

Play It One More Time

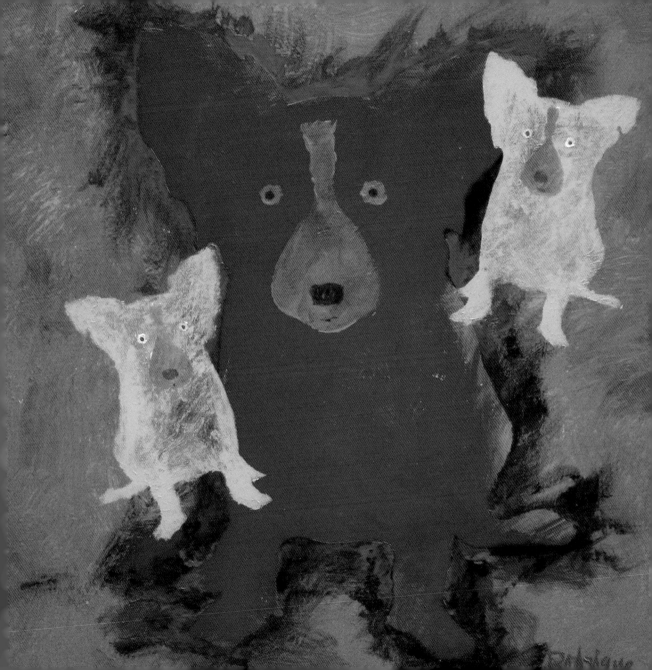

The Red Hot Reunion

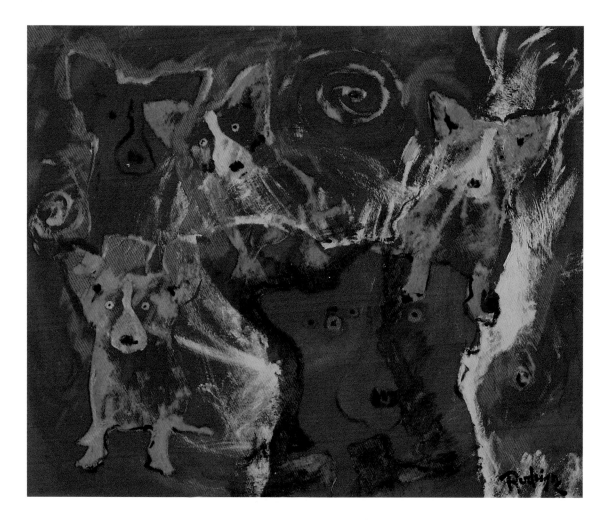

223

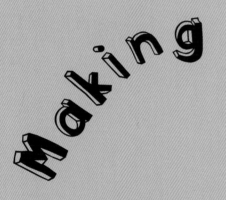

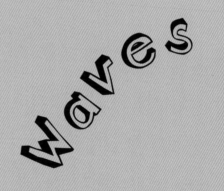

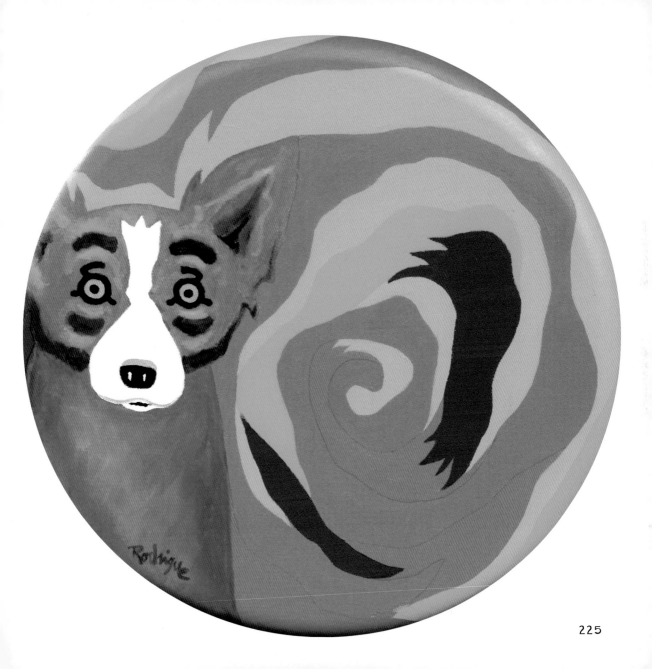

Fall Colors for All

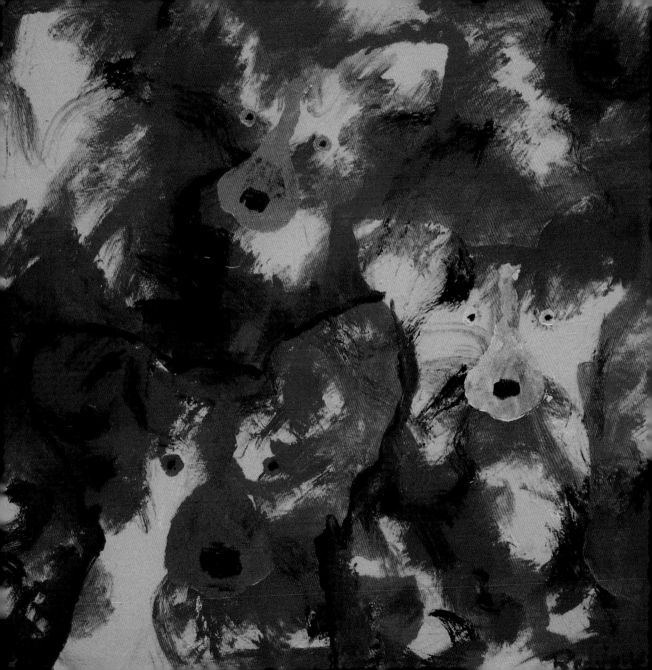

When the Le v e Fal l
a
s

a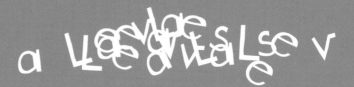

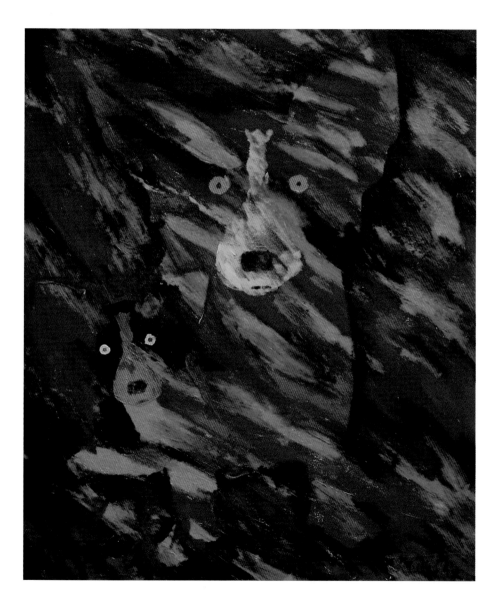

UNCLE BILL'S CHILDREN

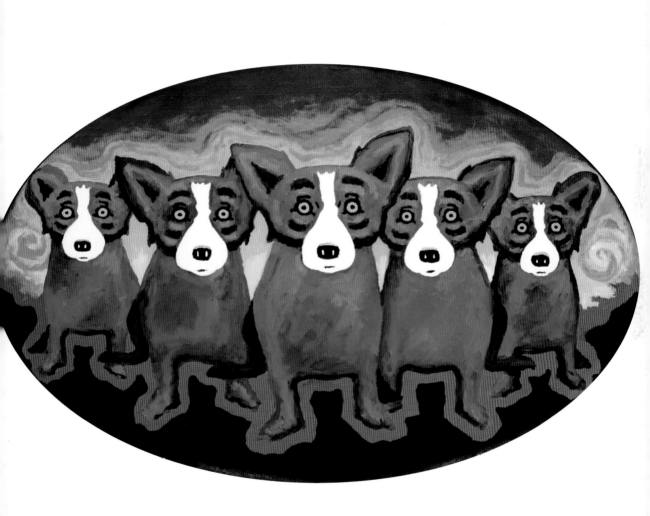

Five of a Kind

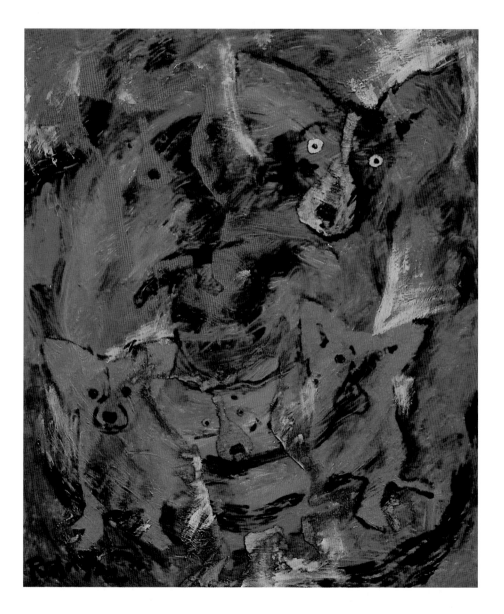

233

You

Would

Think

We

Are

the

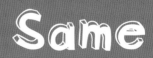

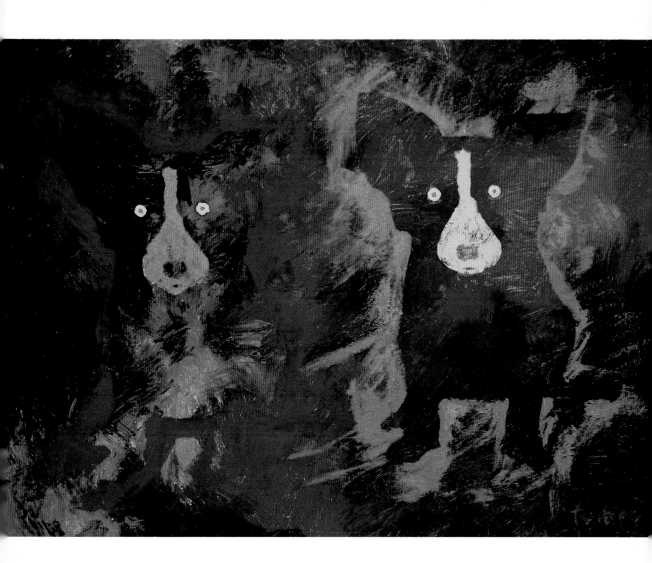

235

Three

Little

Pigs

We're Not

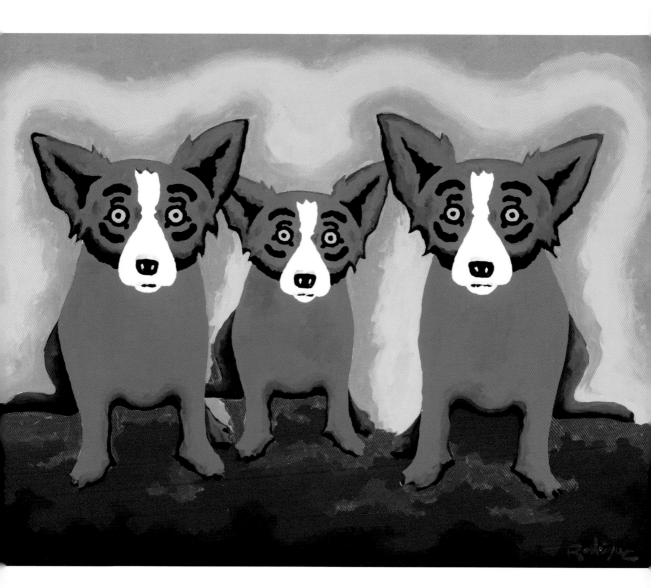

I Look Different

Close-up

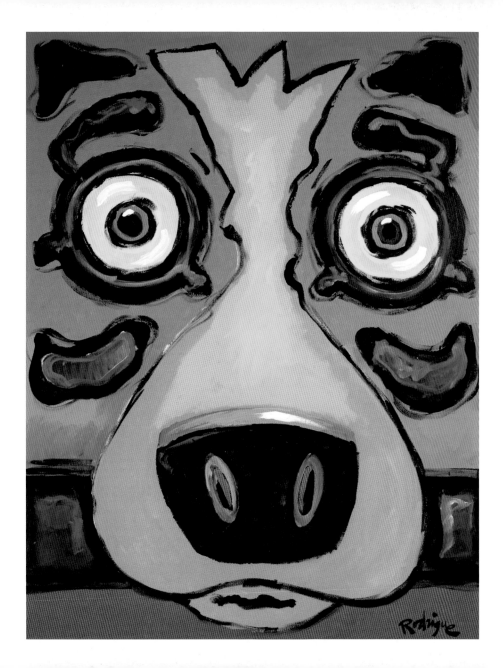

239

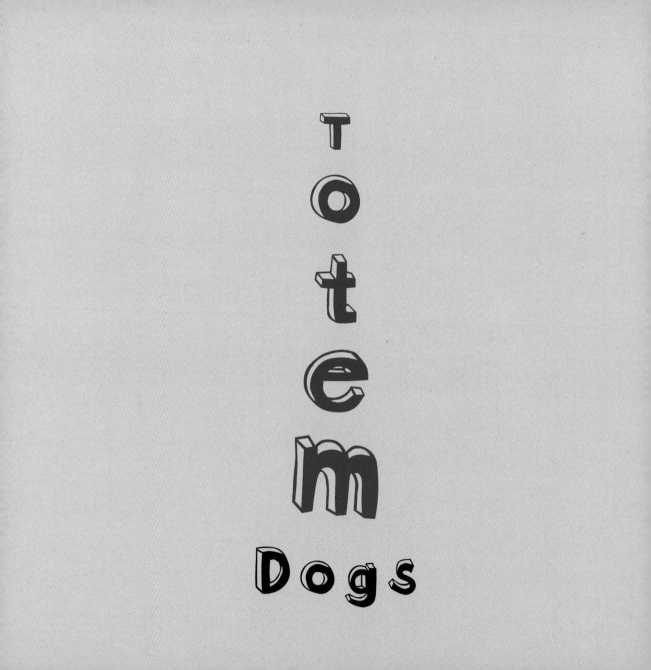

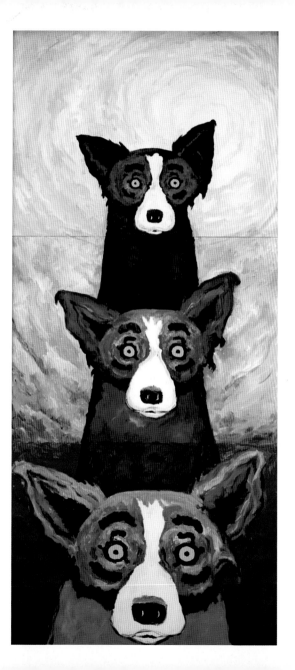

241

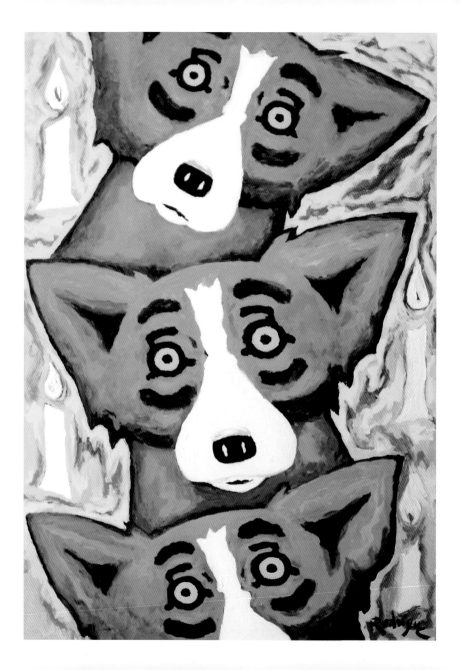

243

Warm Dreams for a Cool Night

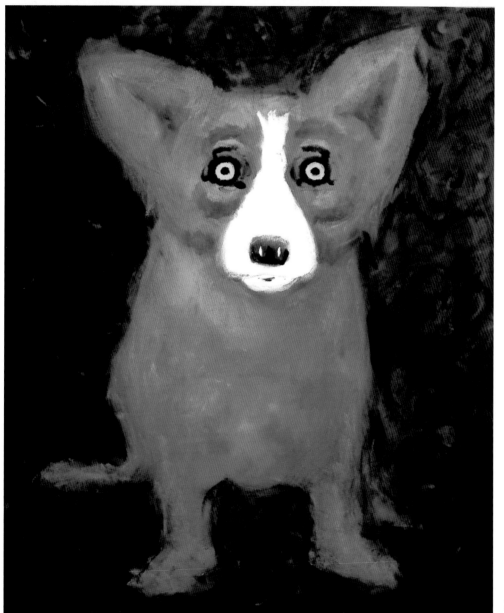

245

Spring Is Coming

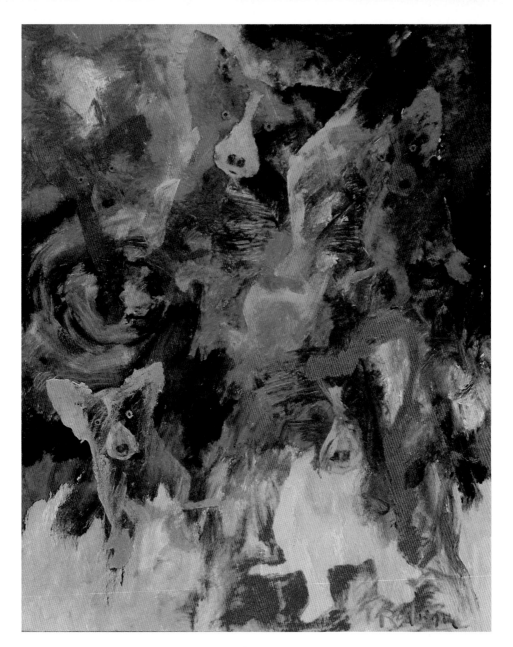

247

We Are Lost

Together

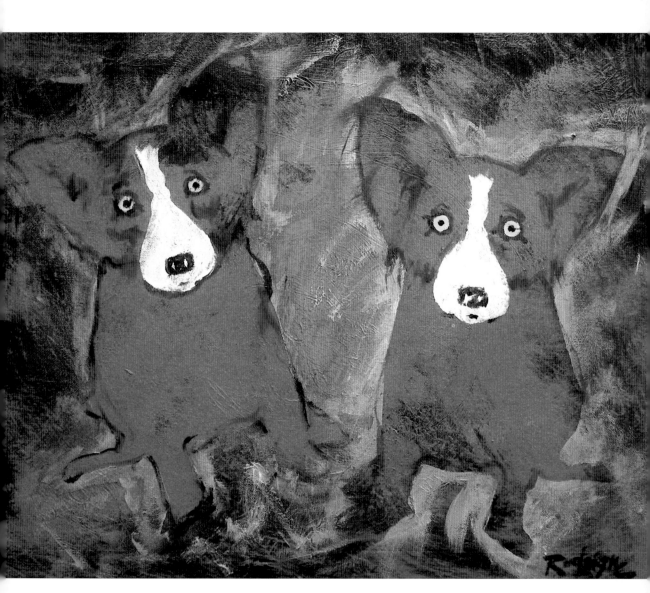

249

Waiting

to Be

Caught

by

LOVE

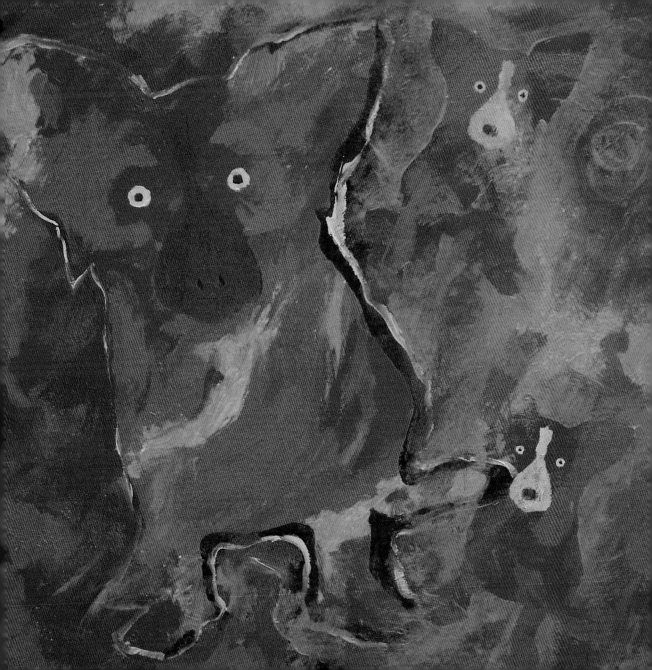

6

The Flowers of Love

Love Me, Watch Me Grow

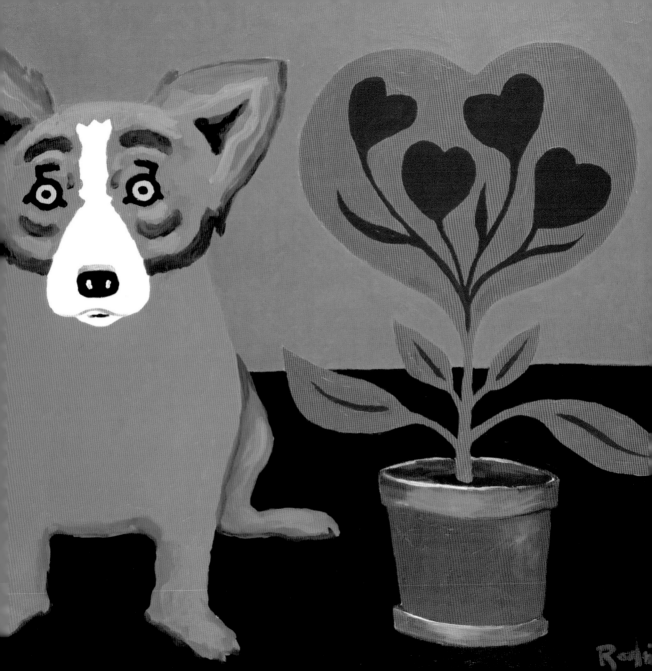

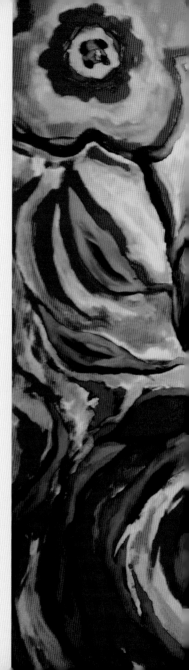

1-800 Flowers

(I Am What I Grow)

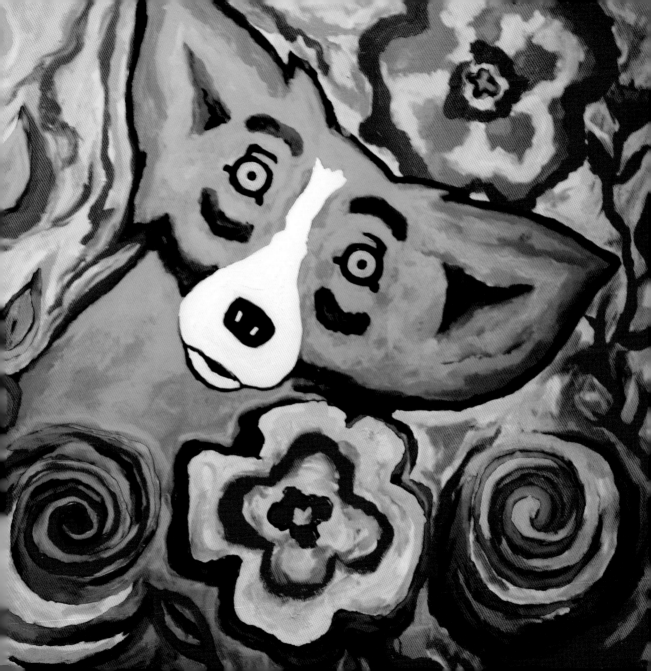

All By Myself with My Happiness

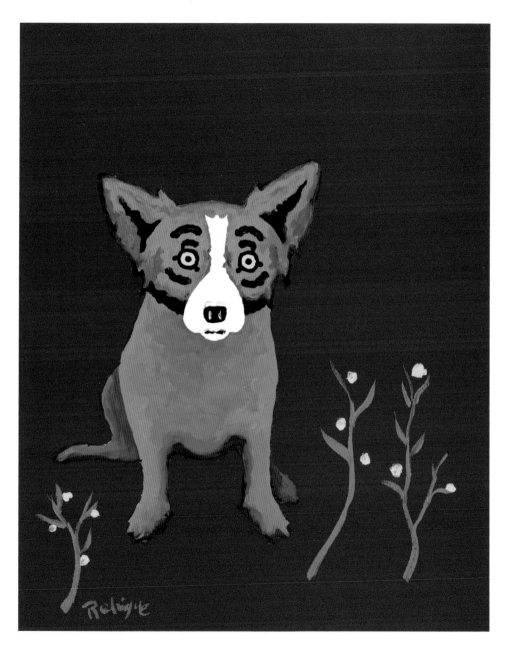

Faith,

Hope

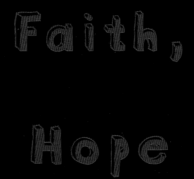

Charity

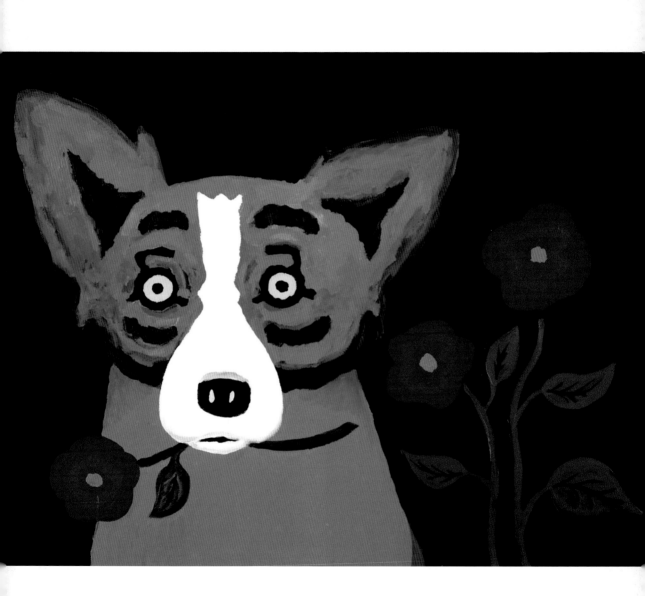

I Grow Flowers for a Living

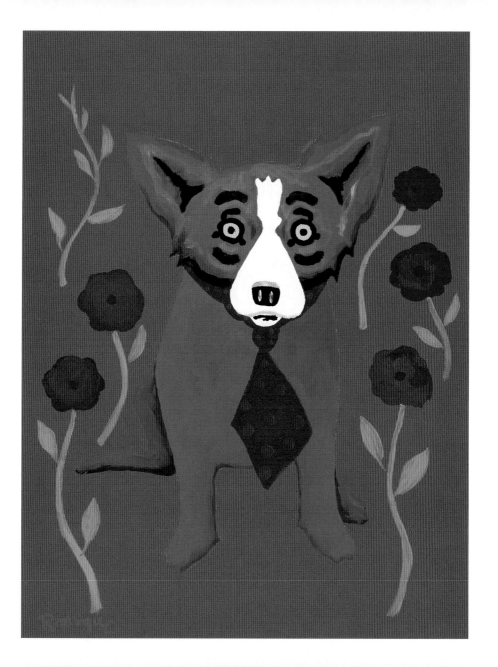

I Planted

THE

Seeds of BeauTy

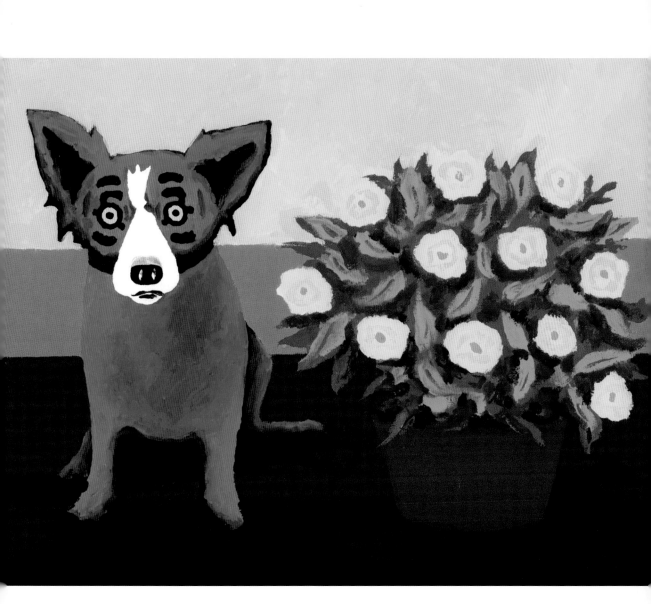

From a Seed Flowers Grow

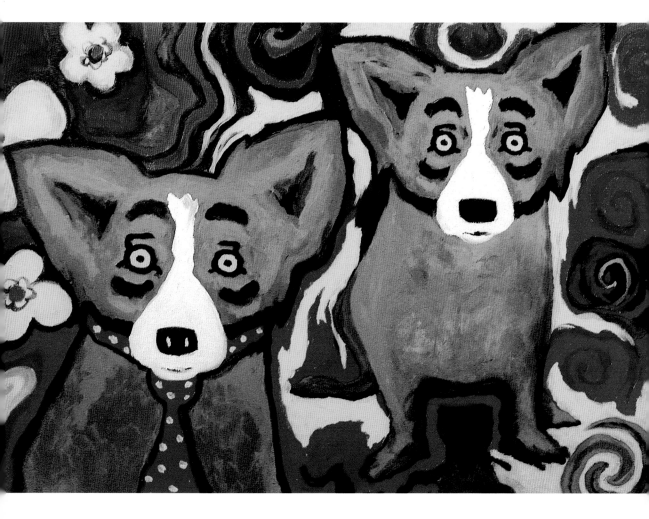

He's Just a

MEAN

Flower Machine

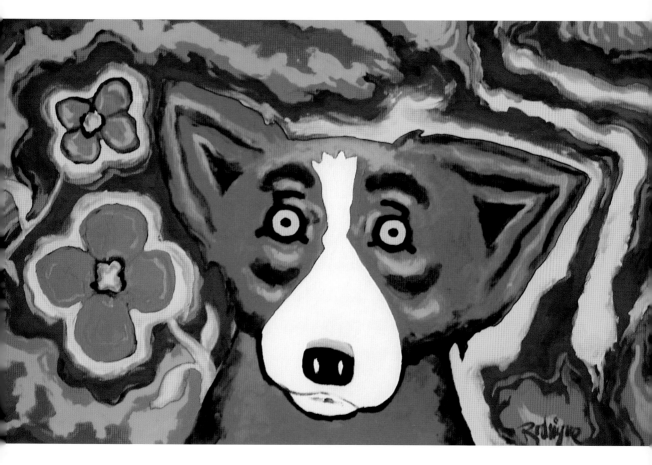

Grow

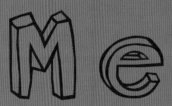e

SomEthin'

Mister

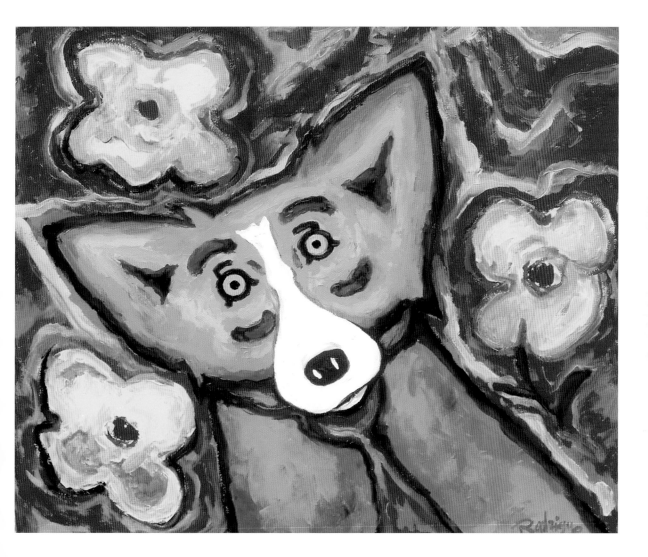

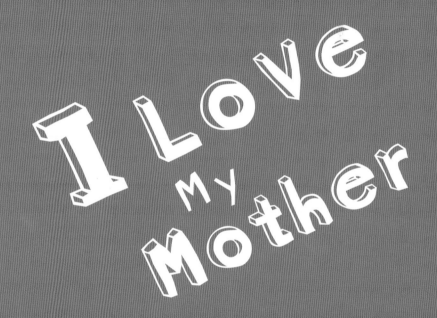

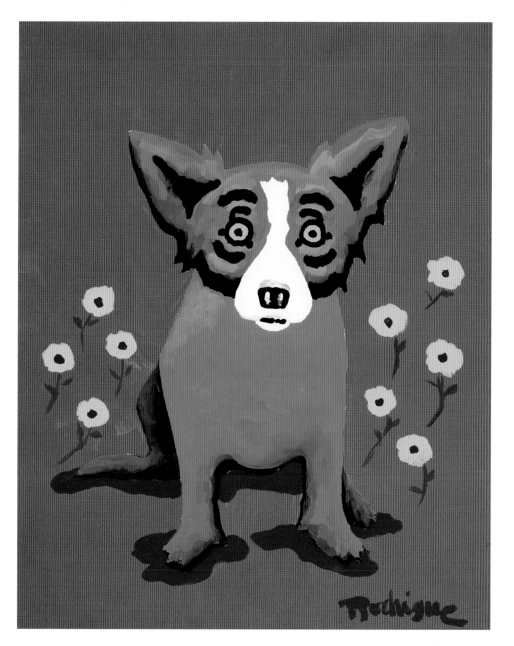

271

Sunshine Over My SHOULDER

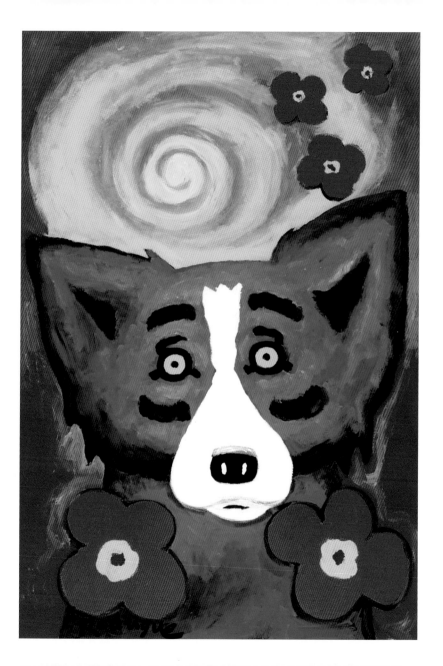

273

Springtime in Louisiana

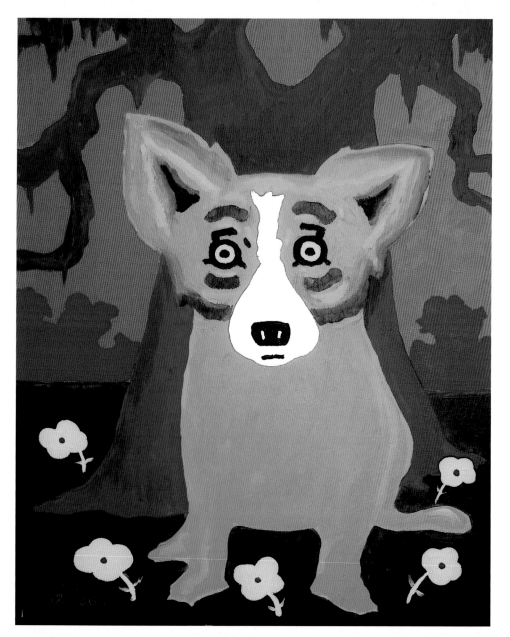

She's

Got

Me

Waiting

with

the

Wallflowers

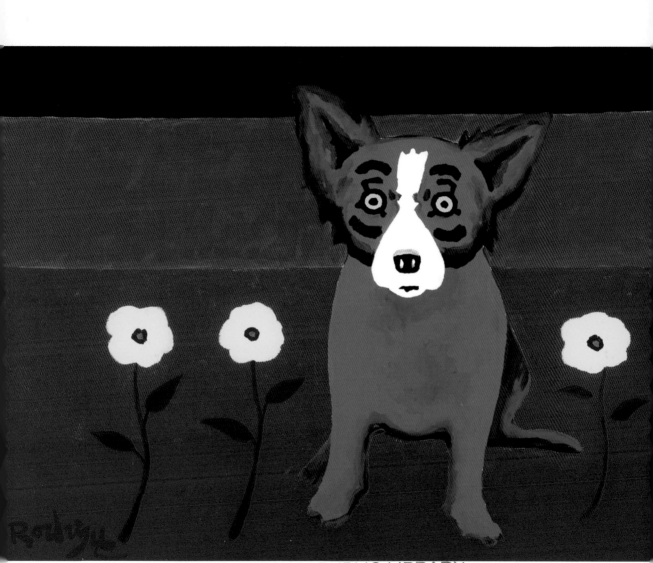

Rodrigue

277

She Took My Heart for a Loop When She

Away

She Threw Me for a

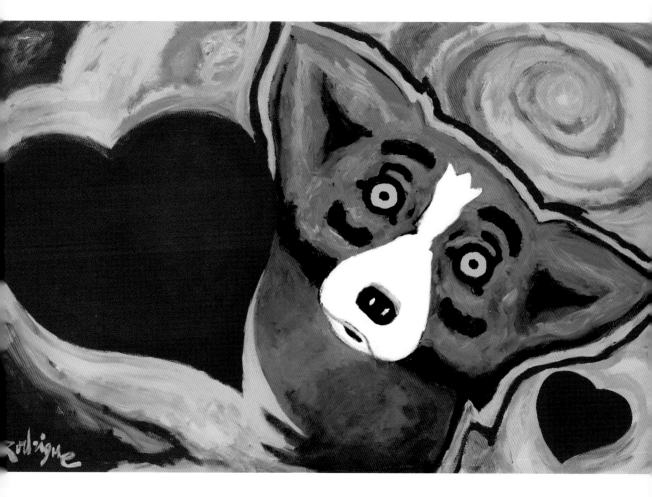

I Sent My Blues

Back to Her

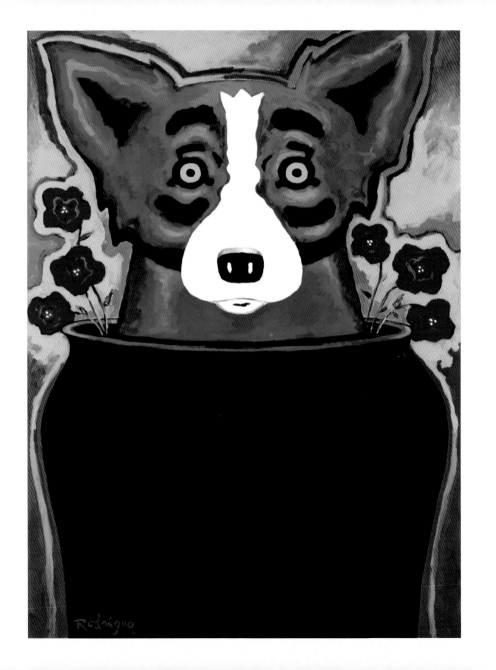

Hawaiian Blues

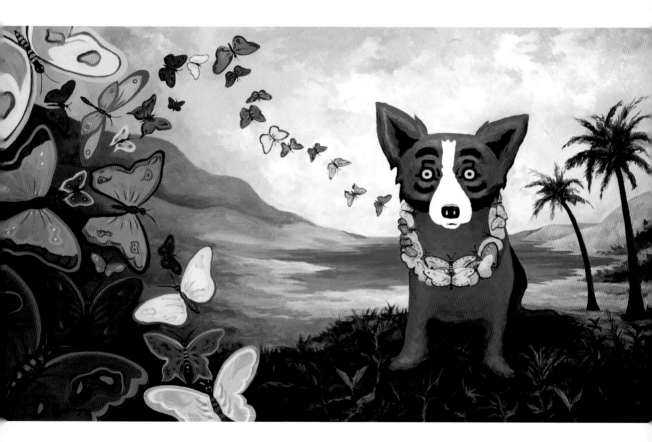

Rut

My

of

Out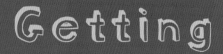

Getting

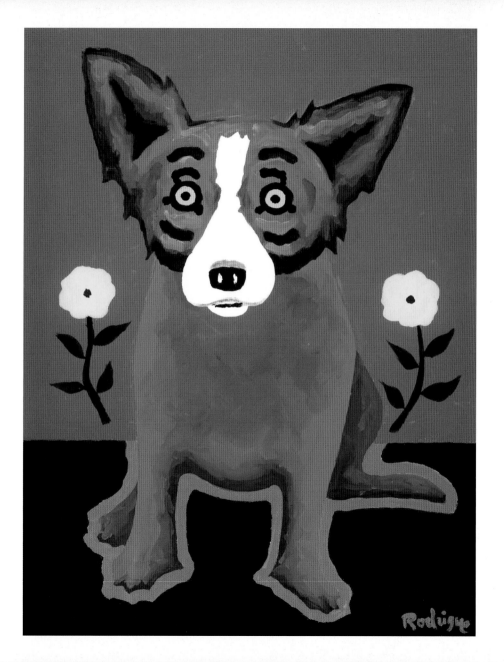

285

Love's Sneakin' Up on Me

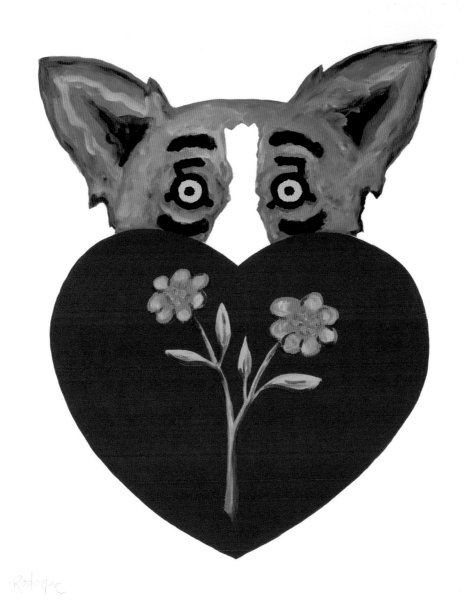

Rodrigue

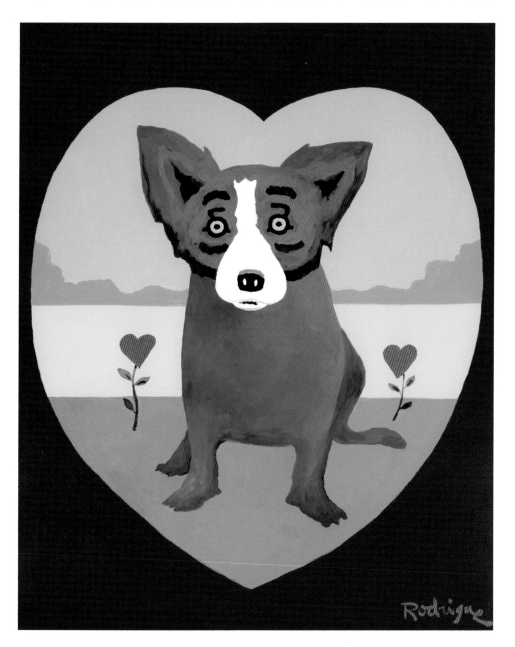

Our Love Blooms Forever

Forever Forever Forever
Forever Forever Forever
Forever Forever Forever
Forever Forever Forever
Forever Forever Forever
Forever Forever Forever
Forever Forever Forever
Forever Forever Forever

(The Day Love Bloomed)

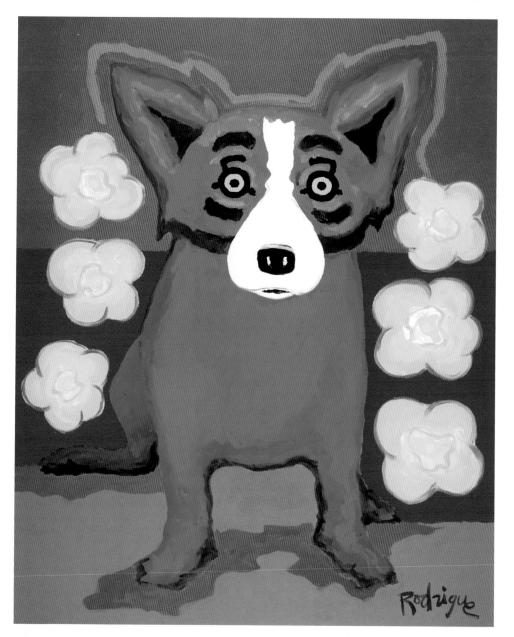

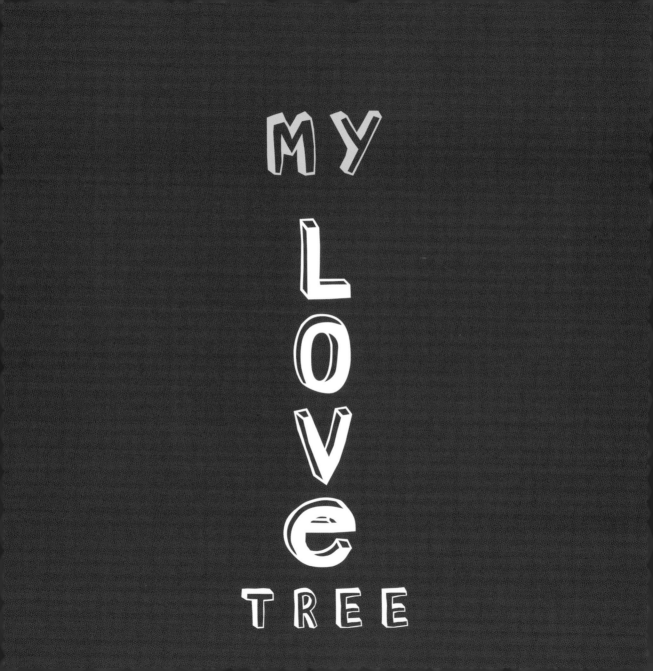

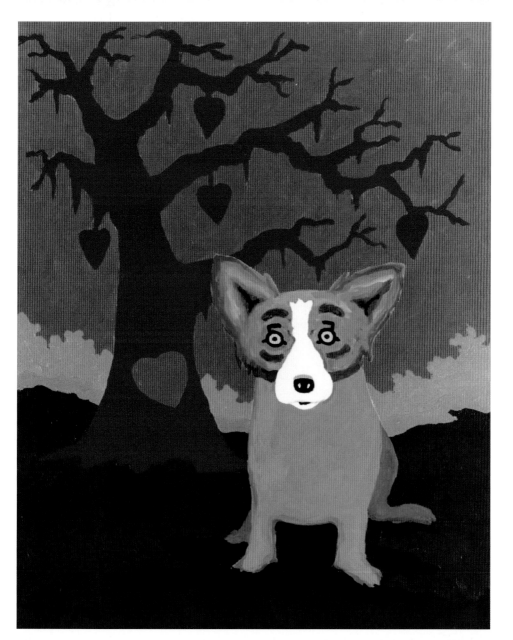

Red Hot Kisses

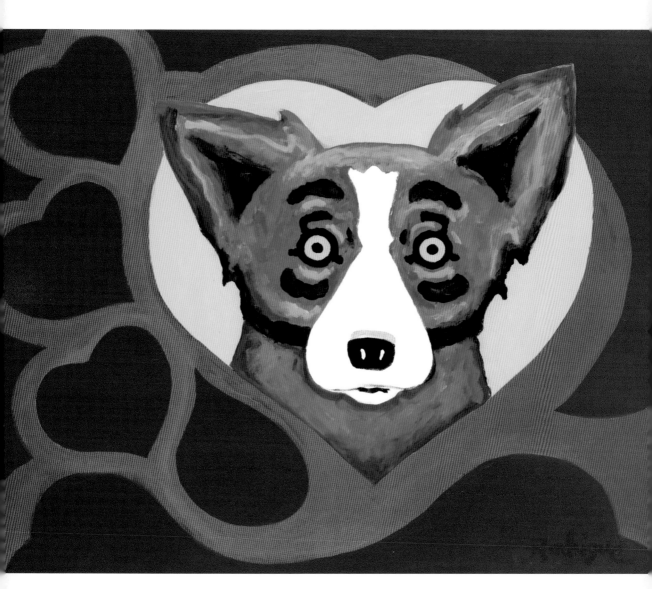

Hot Poppies

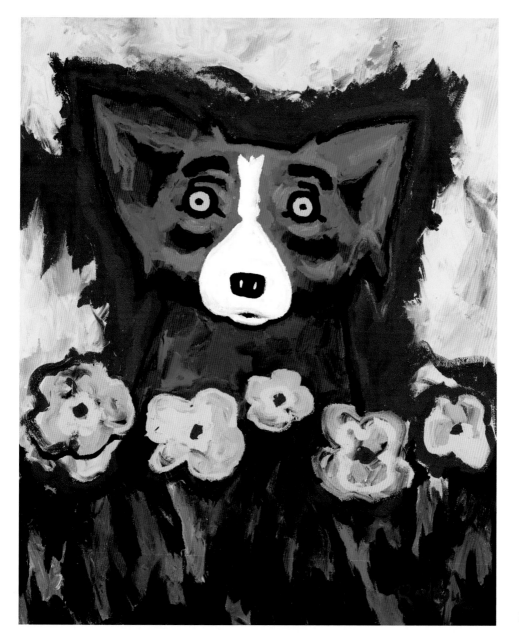

297

Let's

Walk

in the

Flower

Garden

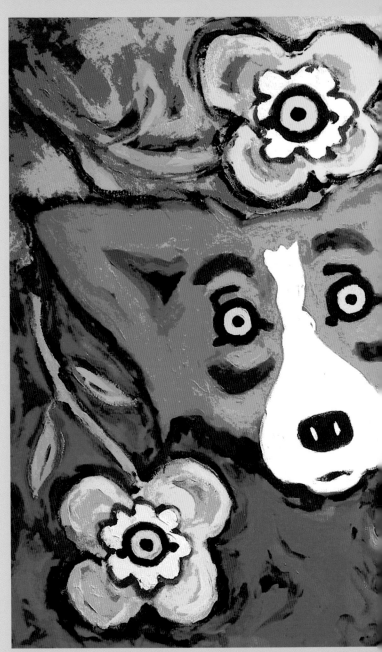

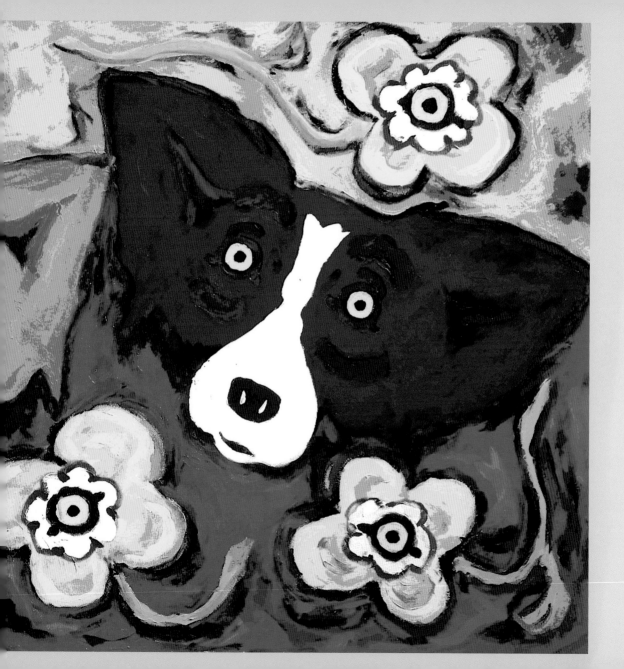

I Cannot Tell a Lie

(Don't Pee on My Cherry Tree)

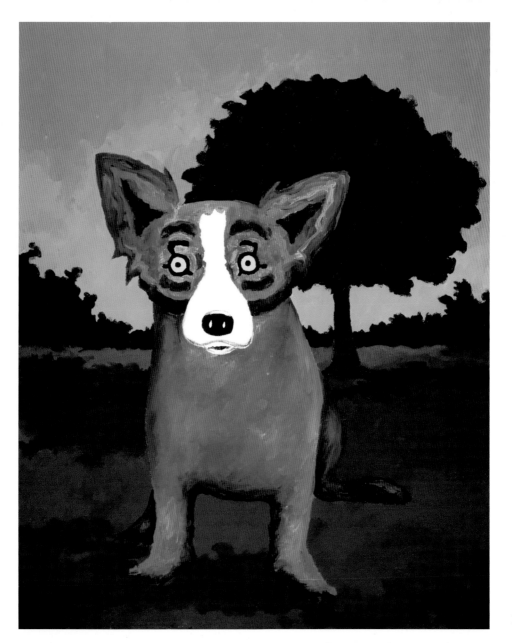

In My
Heart

You'll Live Forever

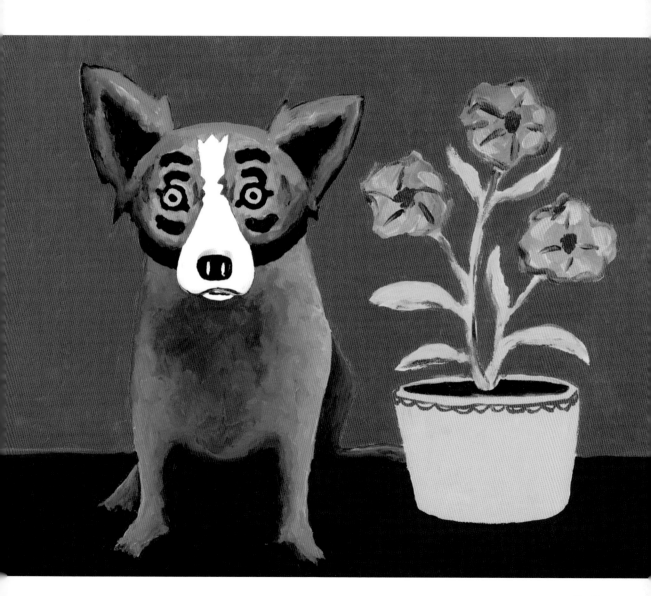

Two Hearts in Love

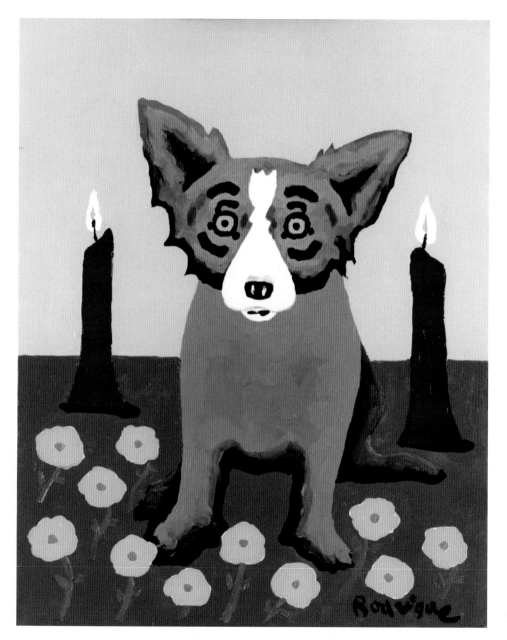

7

A
Woman
Loves the
Blues

She Drove Me Crazy

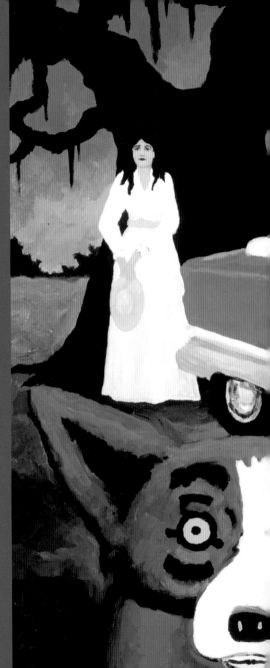

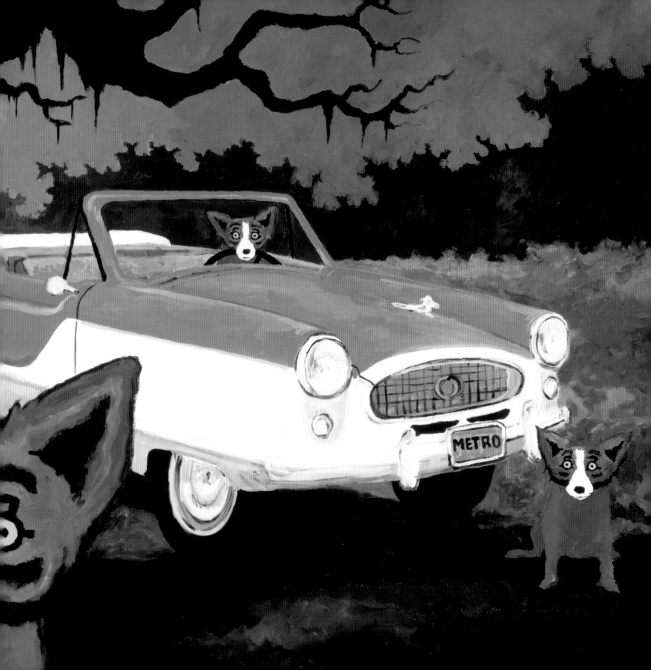

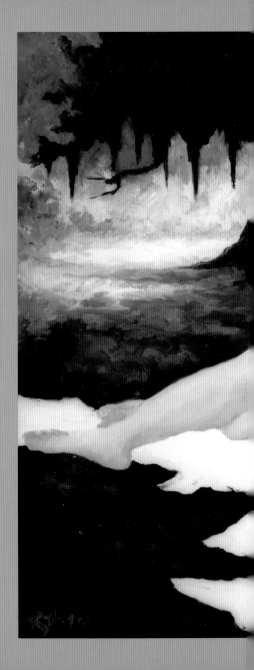

Wrong

Century

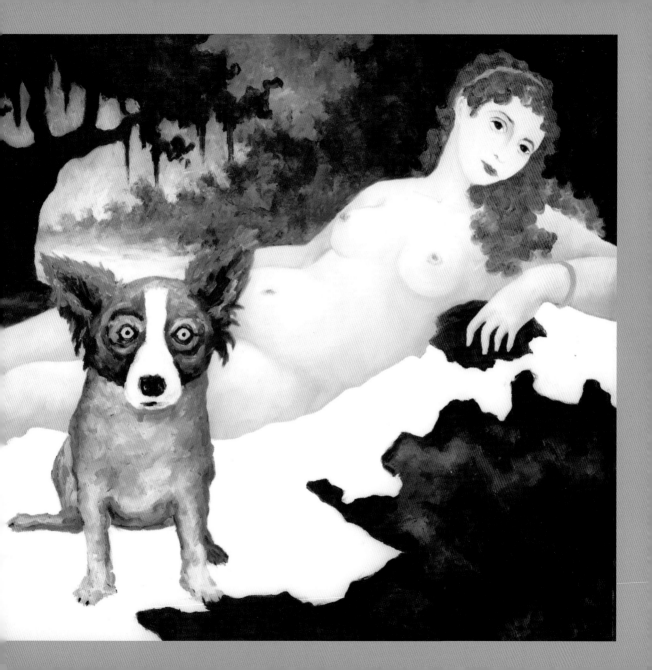

Handle My

HEART

with Care

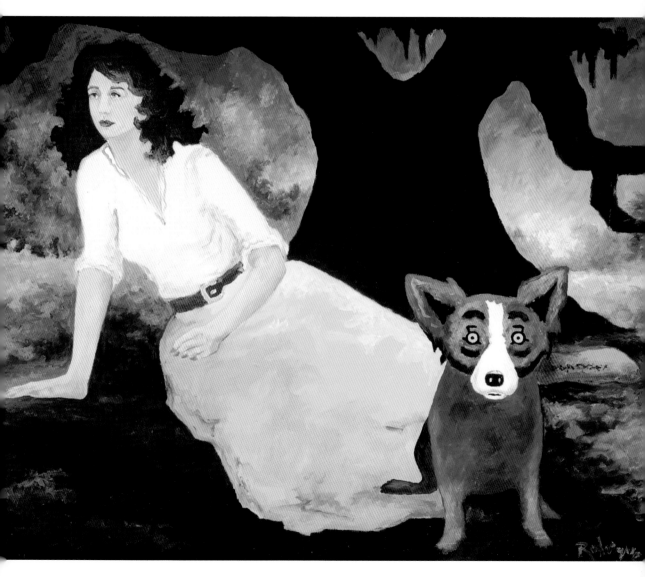

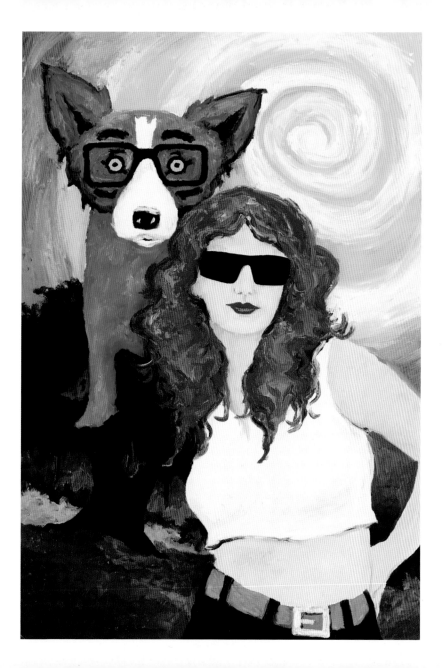

Blue Eyes Blue Heart

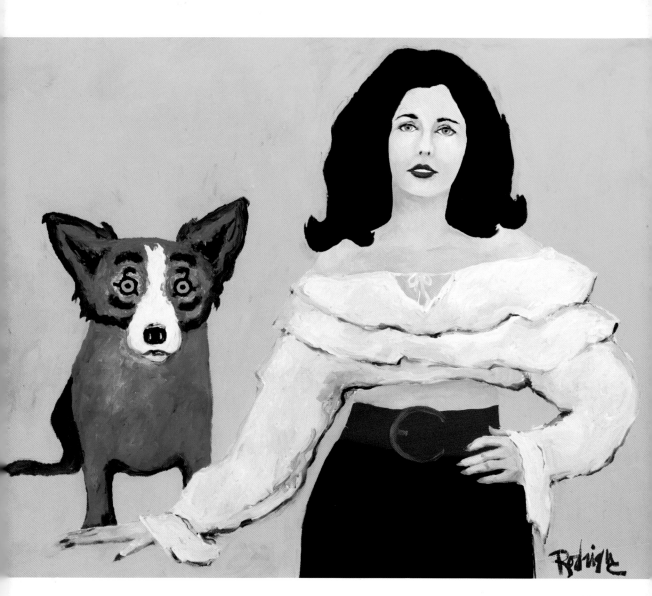

Speaking to the WIND

(I Went to the Graveyard to Hide from the Wind)

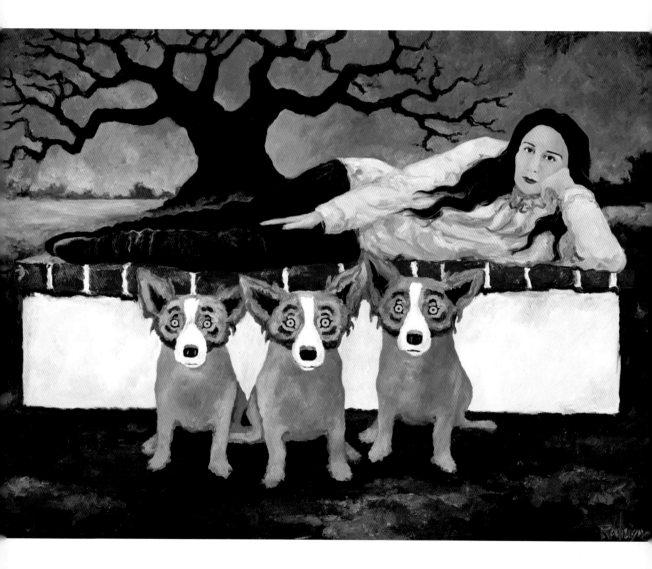

317

She Brought

Color

to My Life

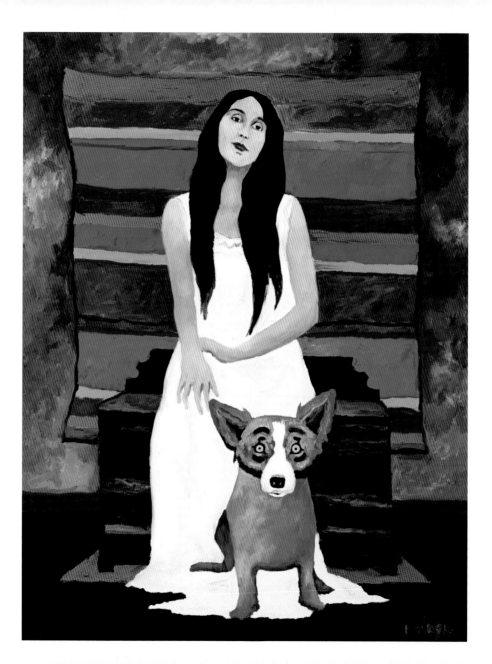

319

Virtual Reality

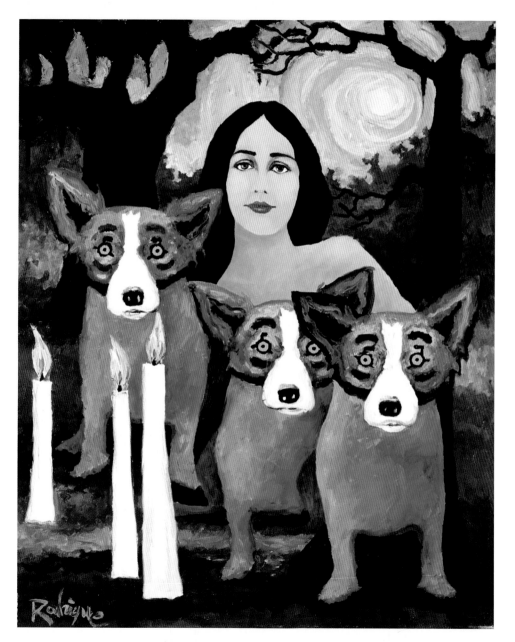

Right Place,

Wrong Time

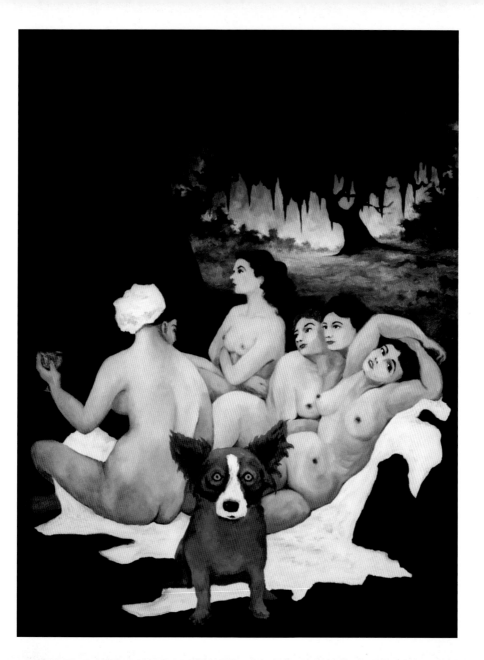

Another

Dangerous
Woman
Crept

into

My Life

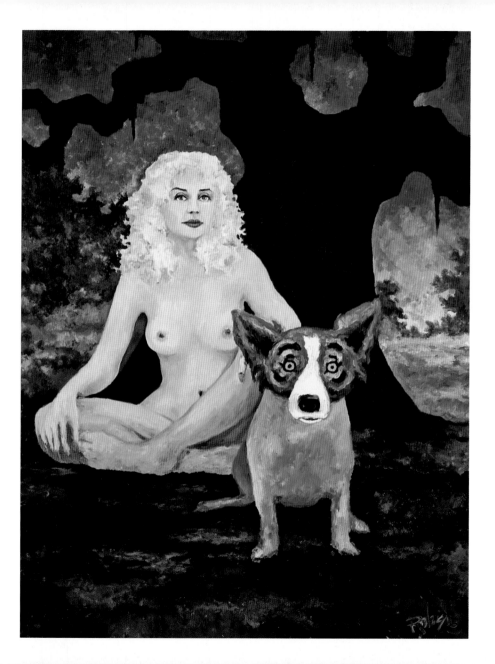

325

She Never

Saw Me

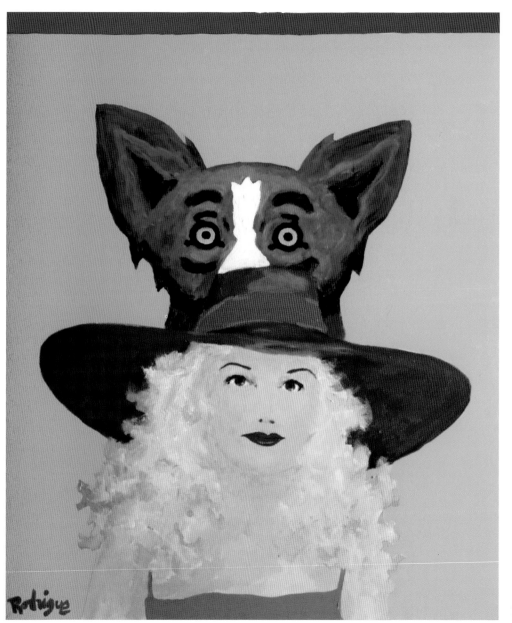

Jolie
Blonde

on My Mind

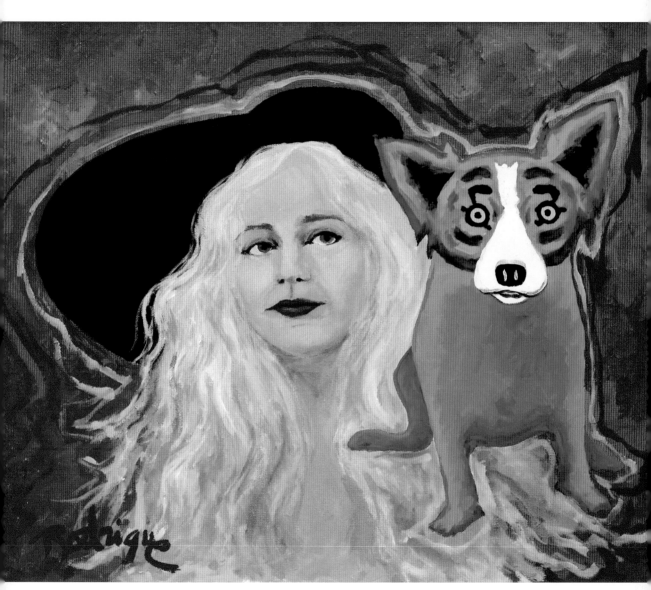

329

Here We Go Again,

She's Got Me

on Her Mind

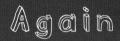
Again

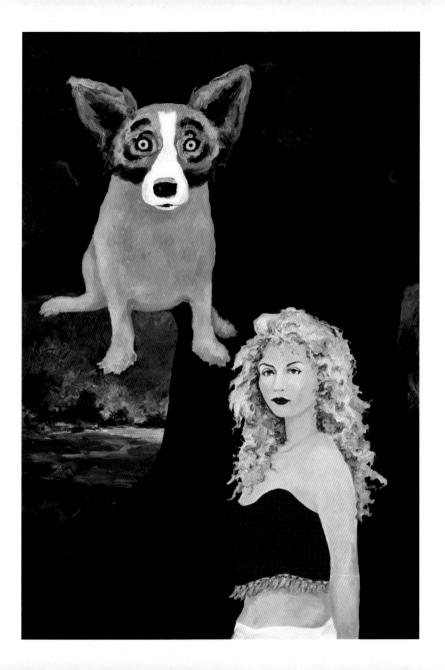

331

Jolie
in the
Middle

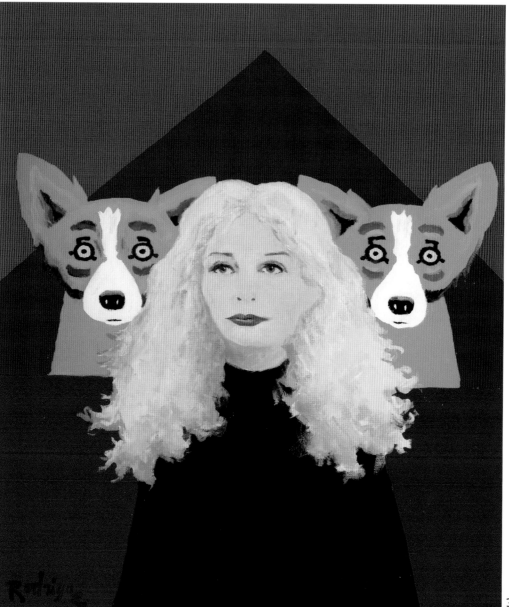

Multiplicity

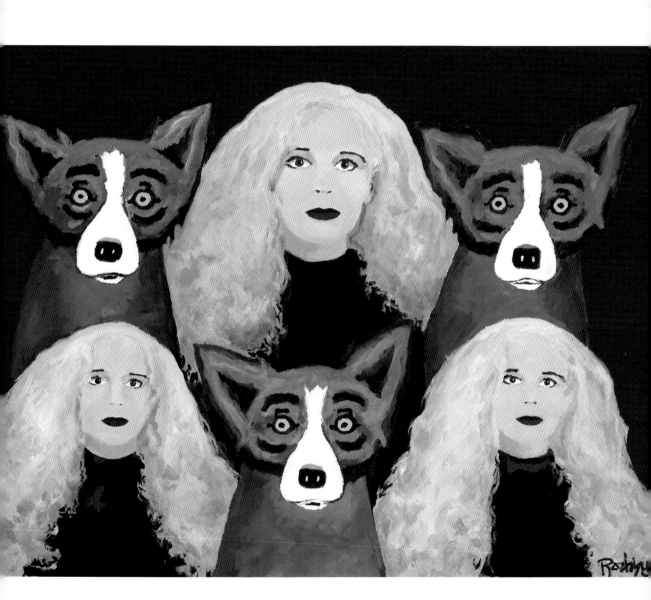

Your Daughter's a Cowgirl

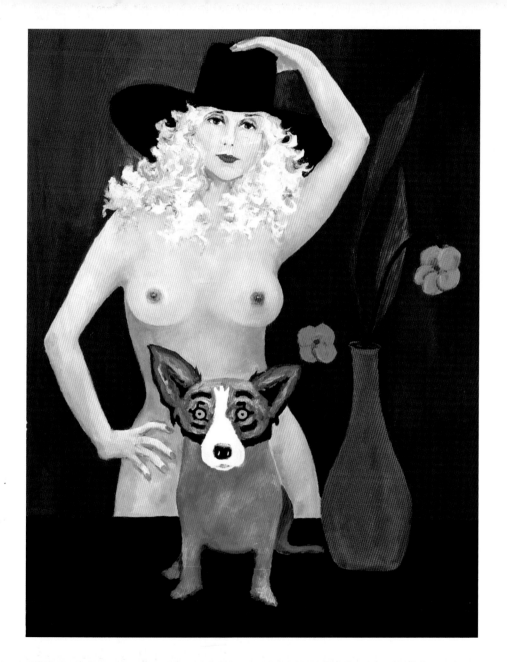

337

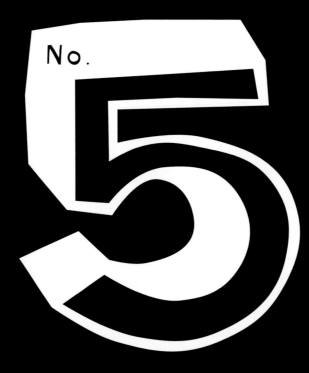

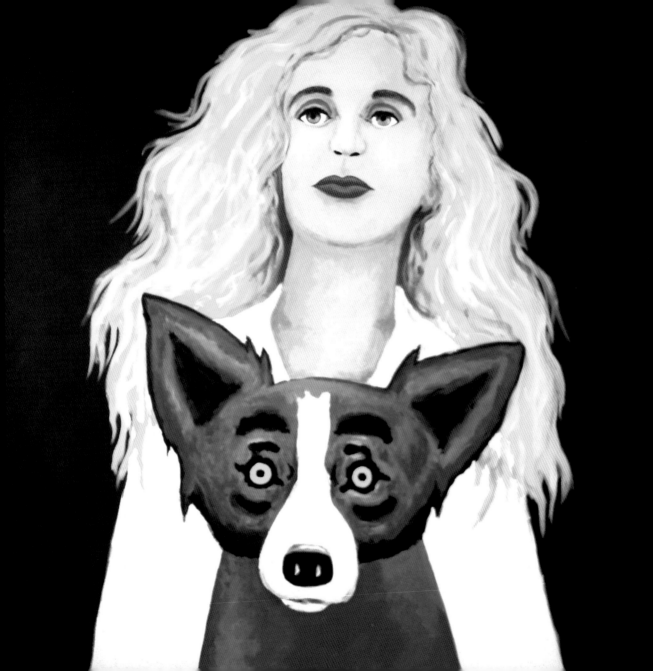

Peroxide

Blues

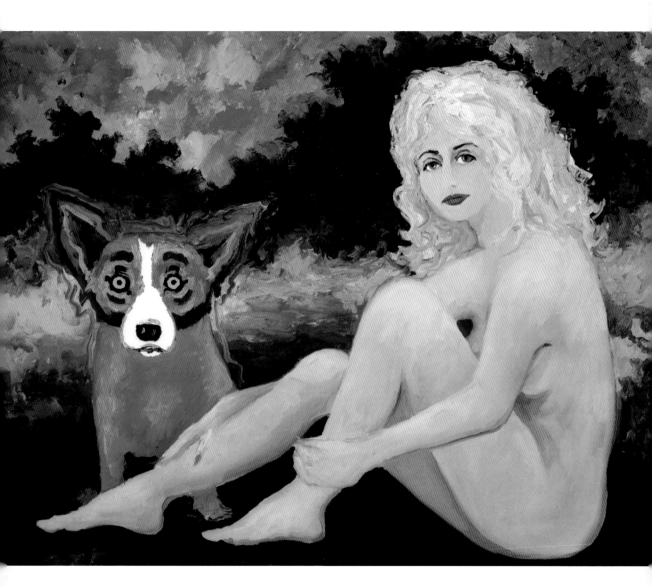

341

Wendy and Me

(The Invitation)

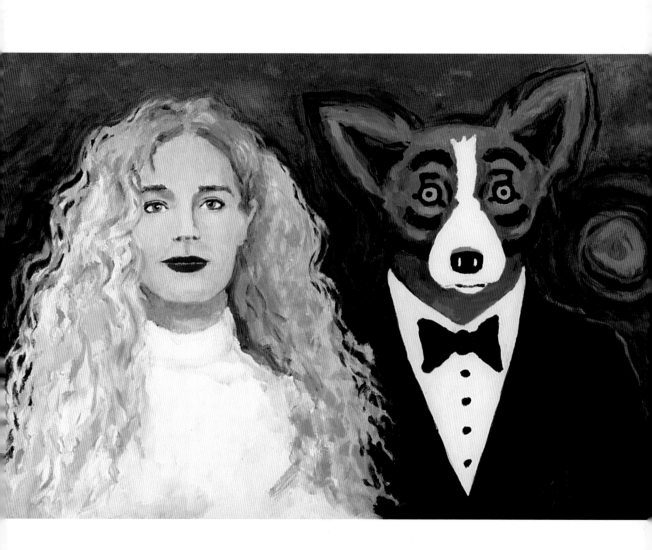

343

The Finish Line

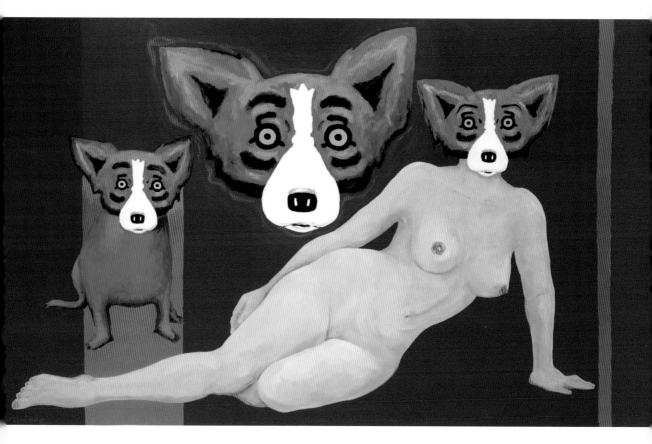

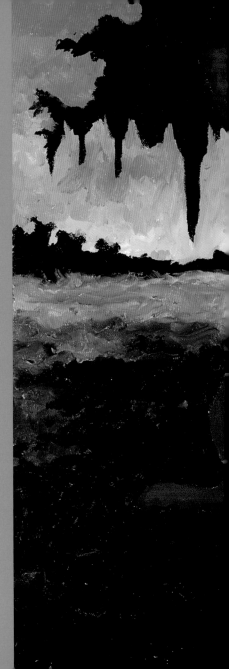

8

A
Dog of a
Different
Color

Lipstick on My Collar

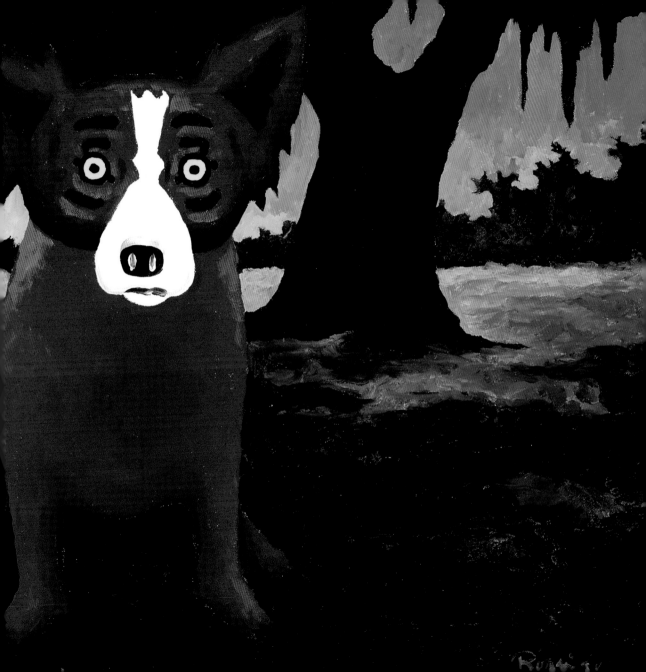

You Never Know Who or What Is Coming

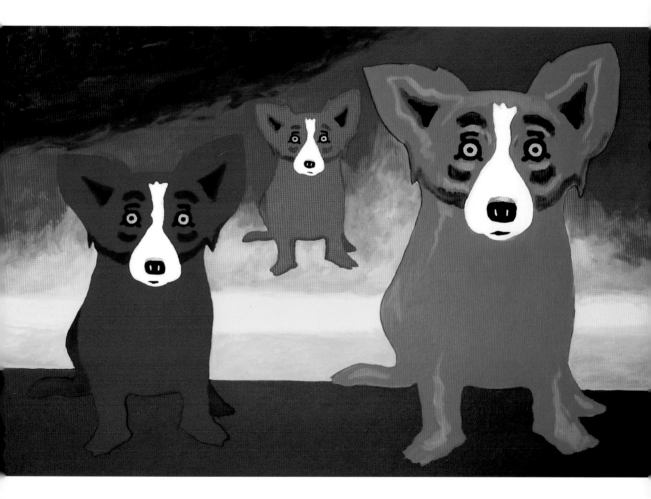

349

The Blues Can Hide

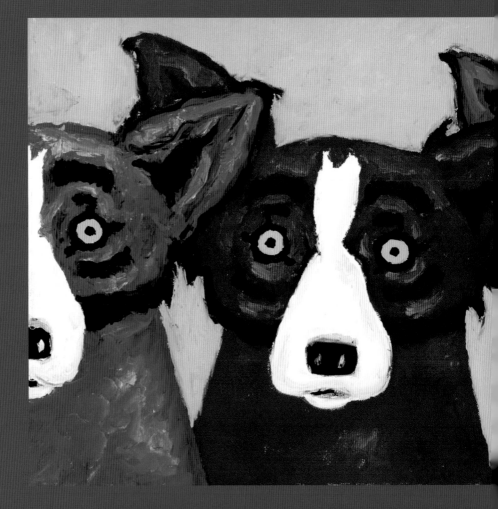

a Bad Apple

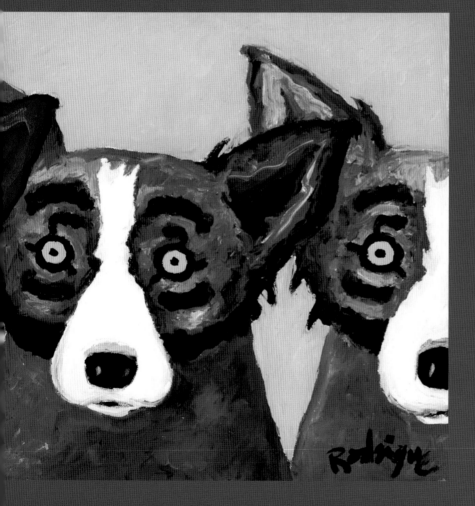

Identical Twins

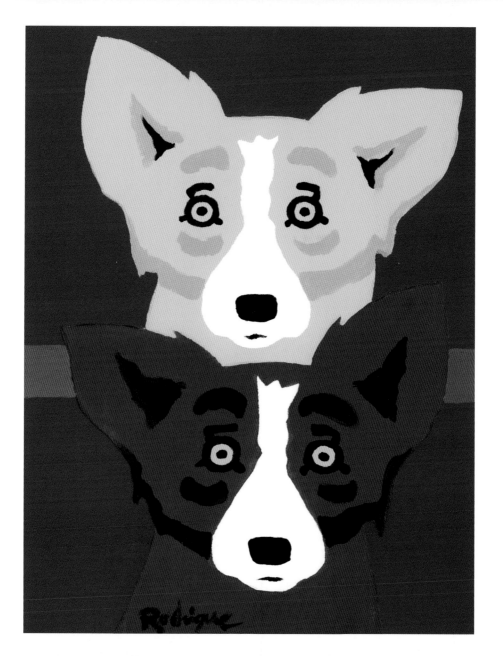

353

My

GOLD

Pet

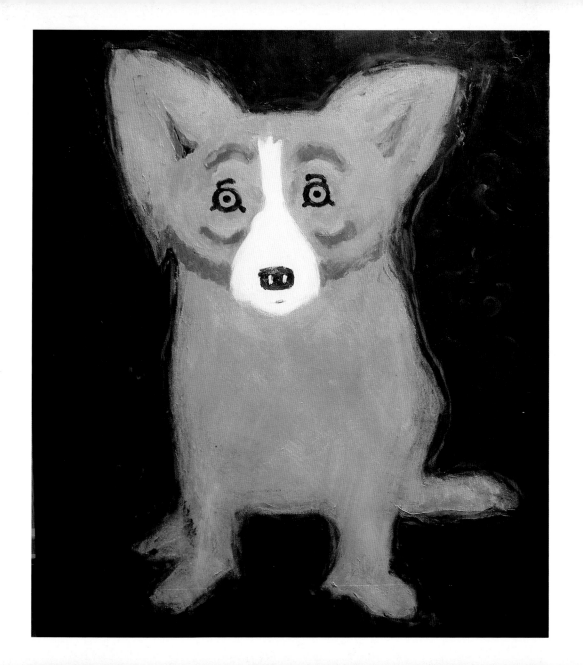

Gold shoes

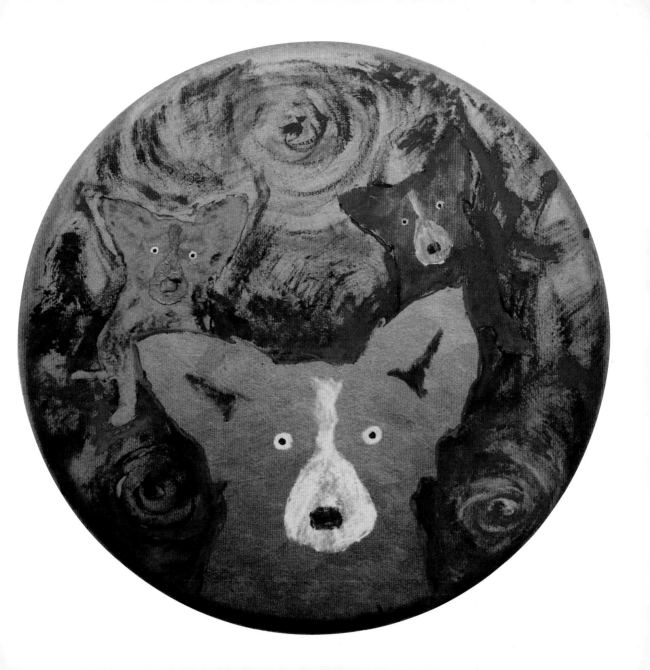

The Andrew

Sisters

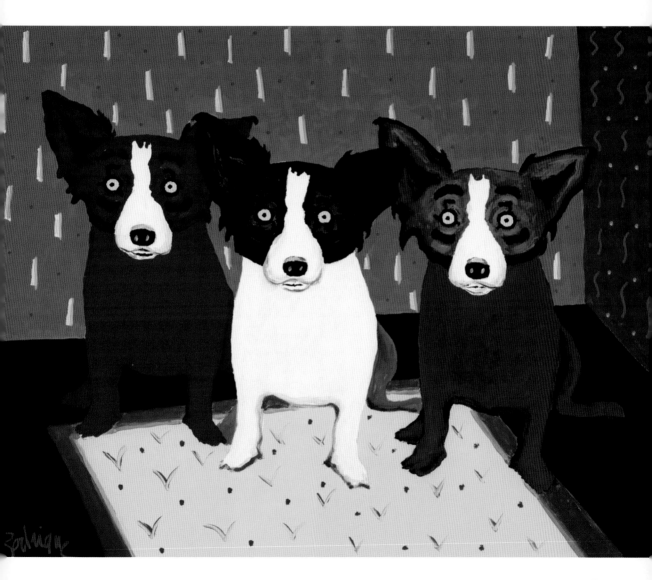

The Everly Brothers

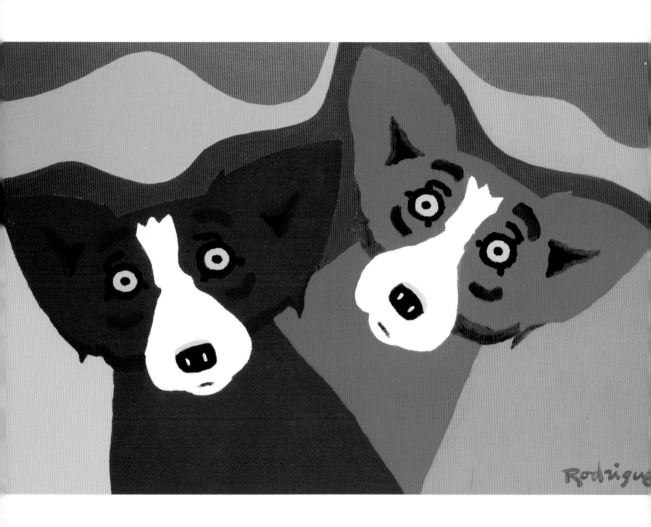

Three
DOG
Night

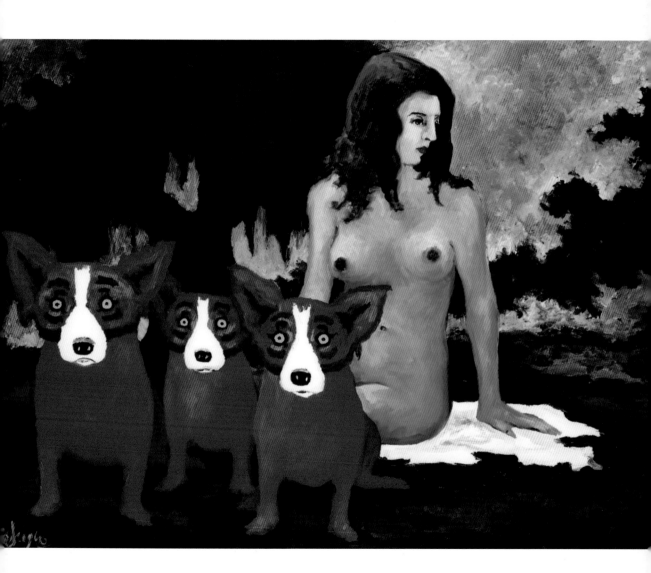

363

Sun Kiss

and   the

Orange

Peels

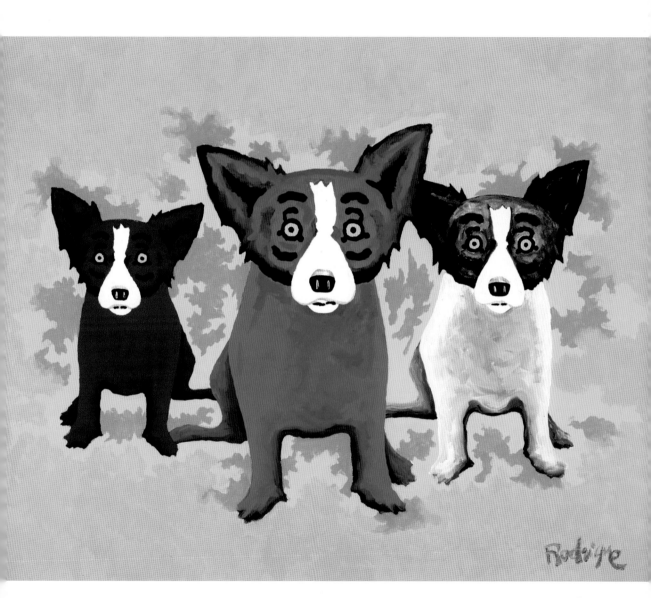

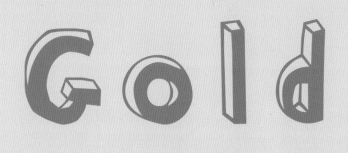

Gold

Blues

Me

Away

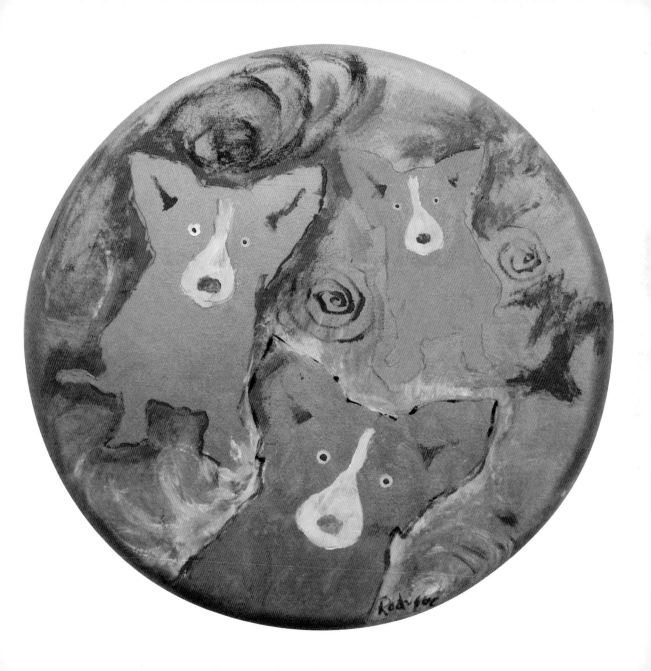

Stars

Out

Hang

Together

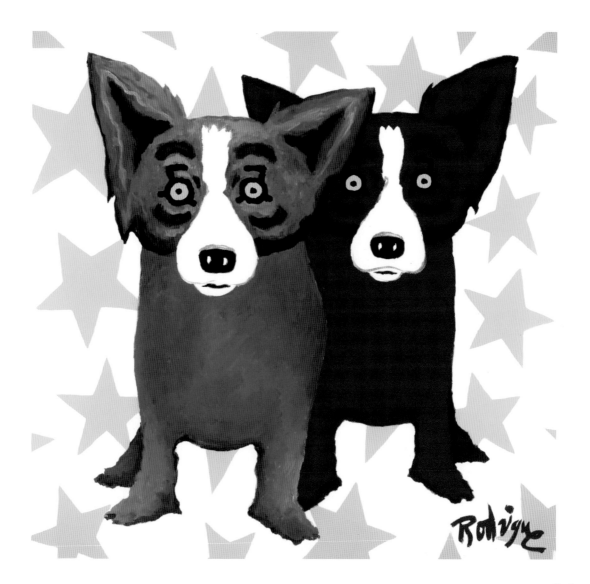

Boiling My
Blues Away

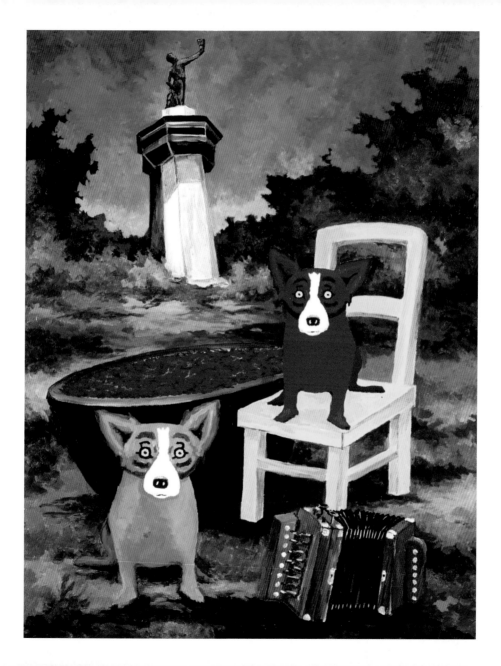

371

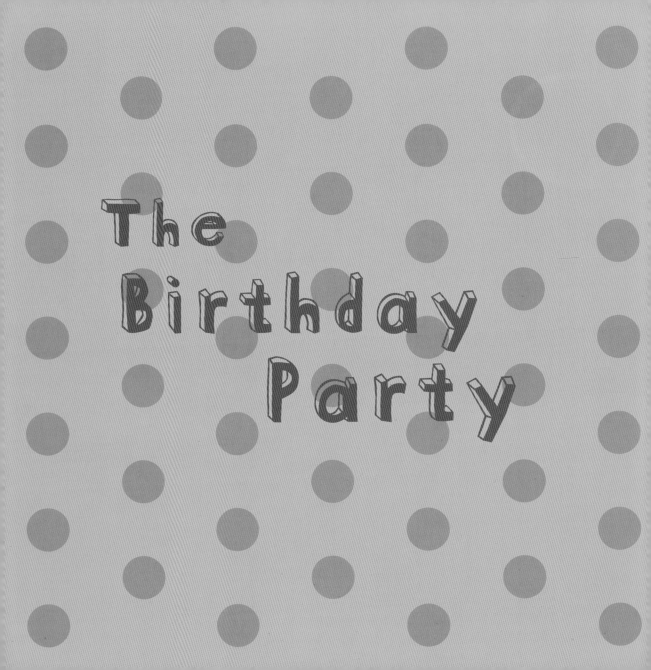

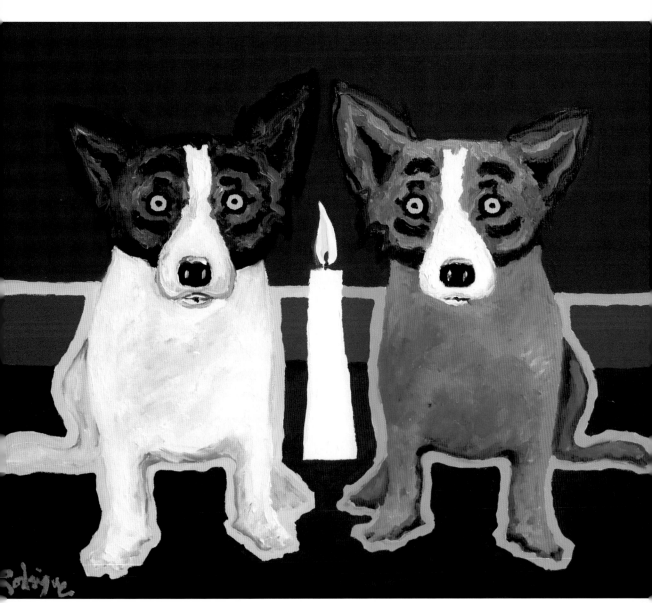

Islands

in

the

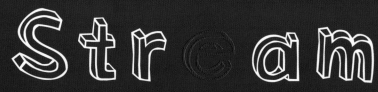

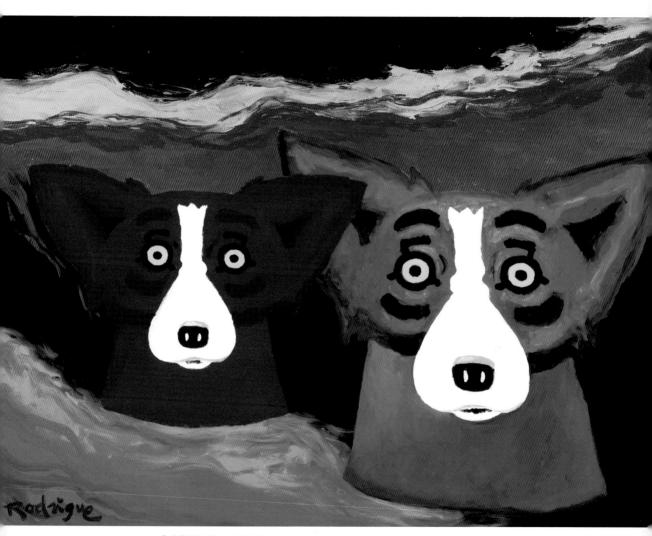

Rodrigue

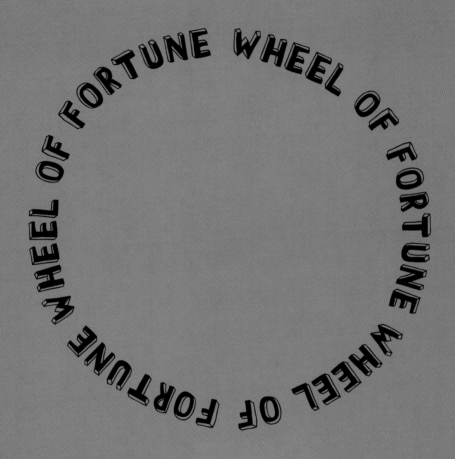

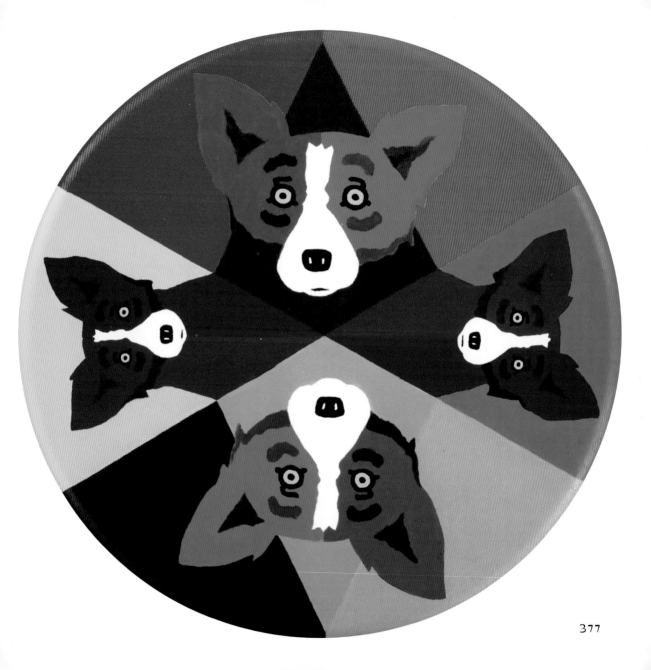

Don't

Show   Me

Your

Colors

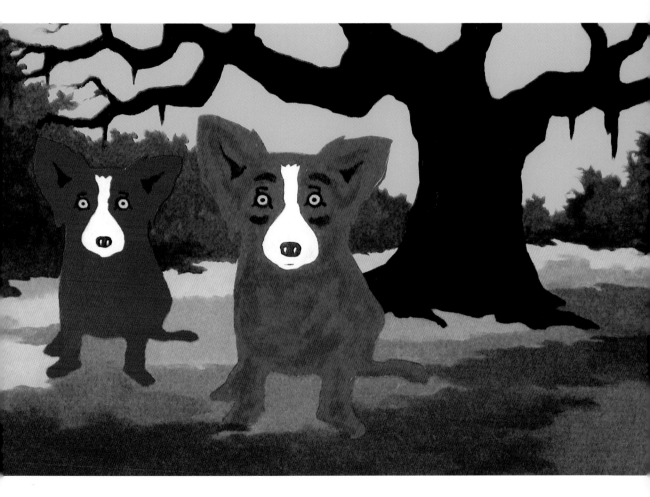

379

Stoplight

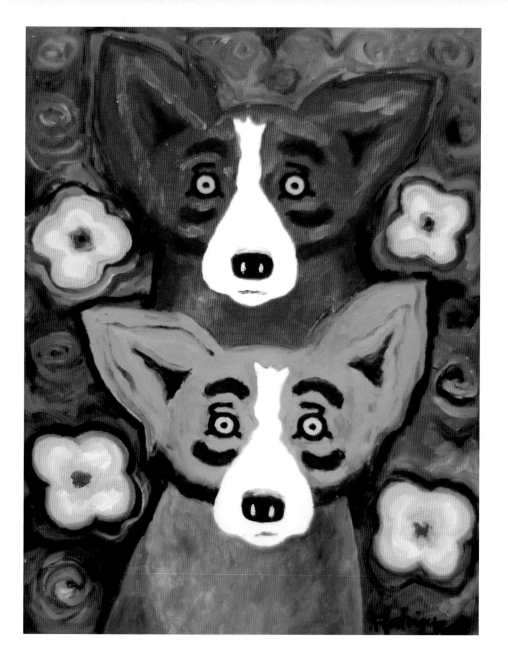

381

She

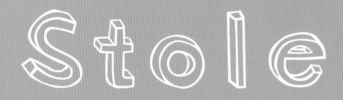

My

Burning Heart

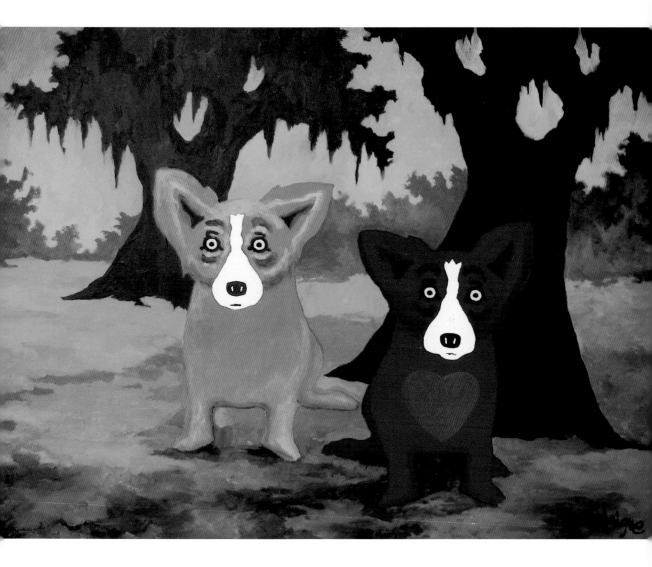

383

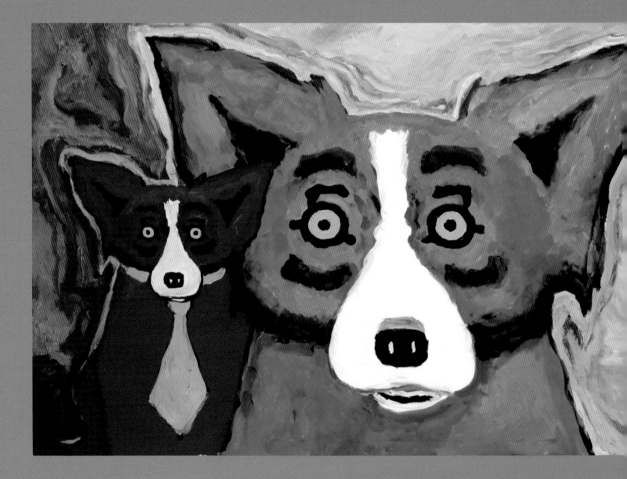

Angel on My Shoulder

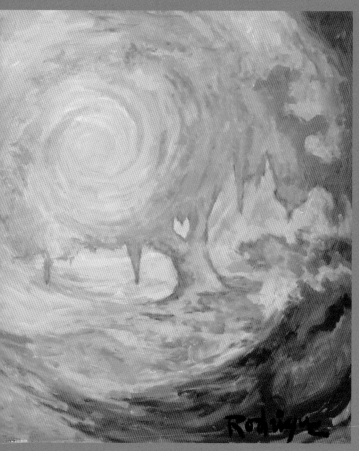

Evermore

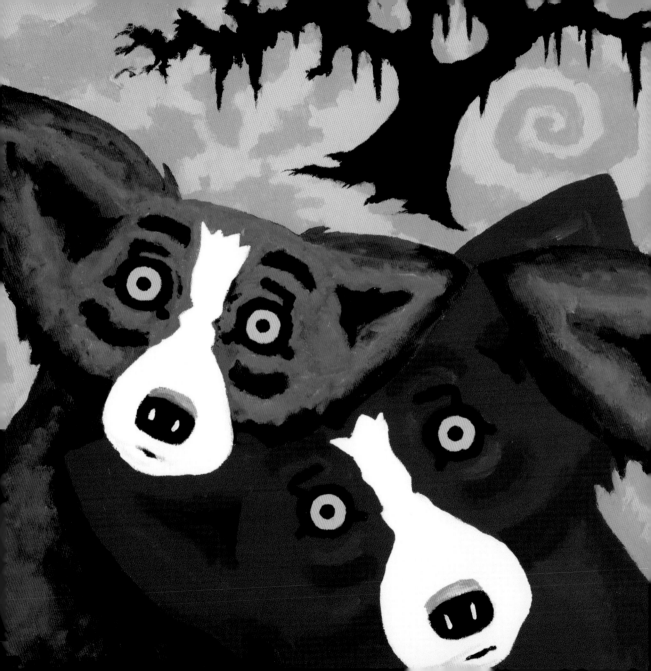

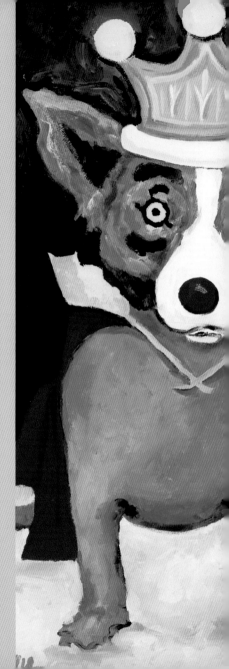

9

Masquerade

I Just Don't Wanna Be Me

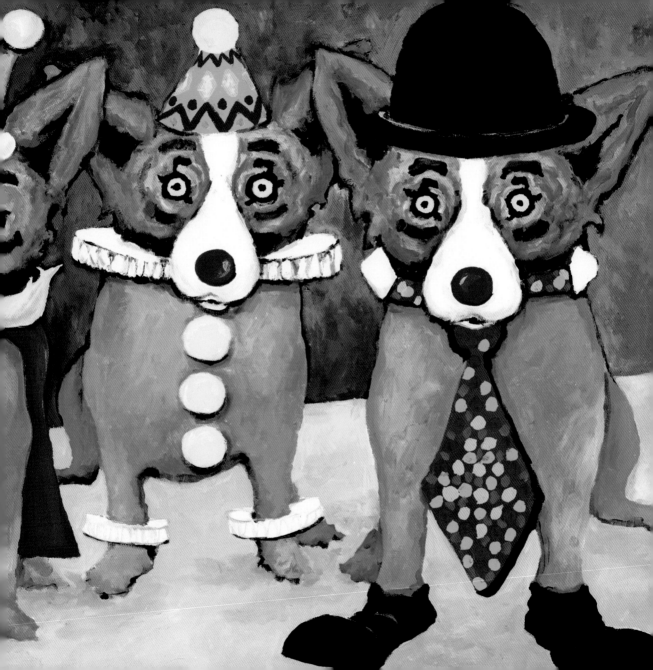

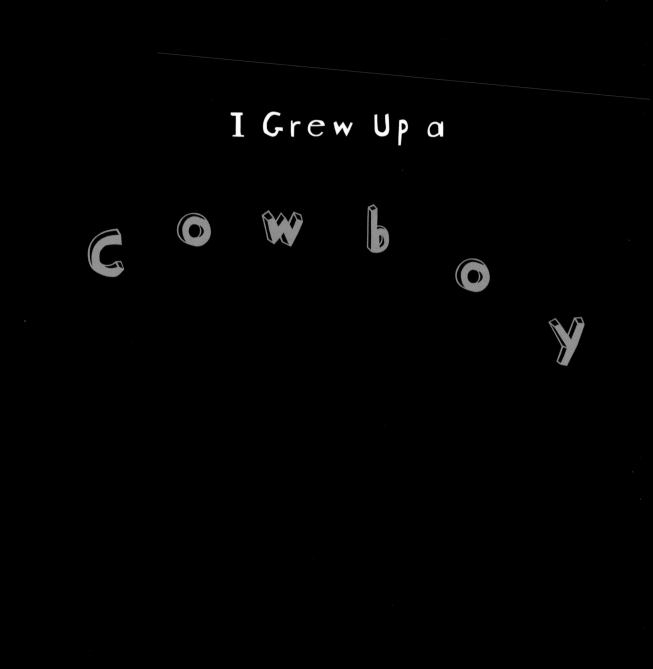

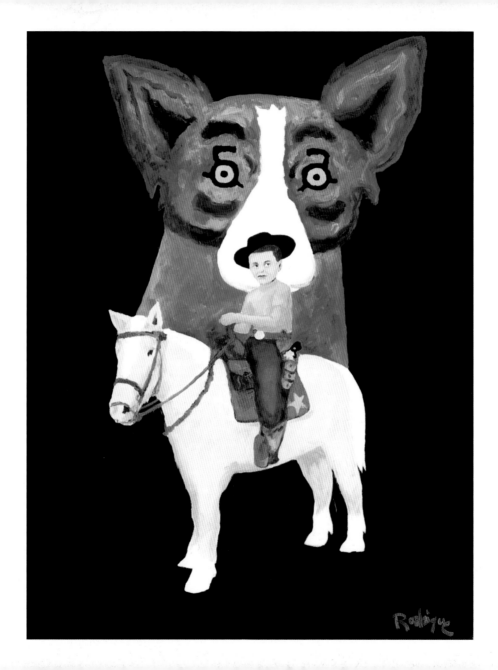

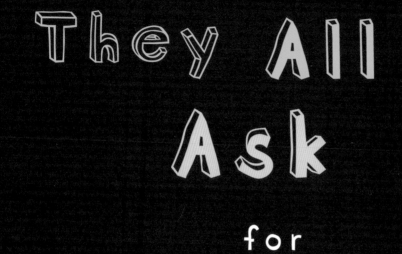

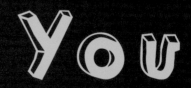

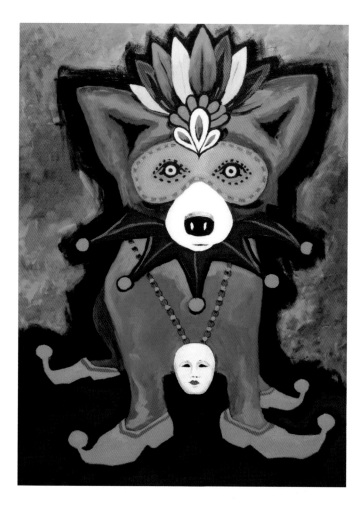

BIG
TOP
DOG

(My Baby Made a Clown Out of Me)

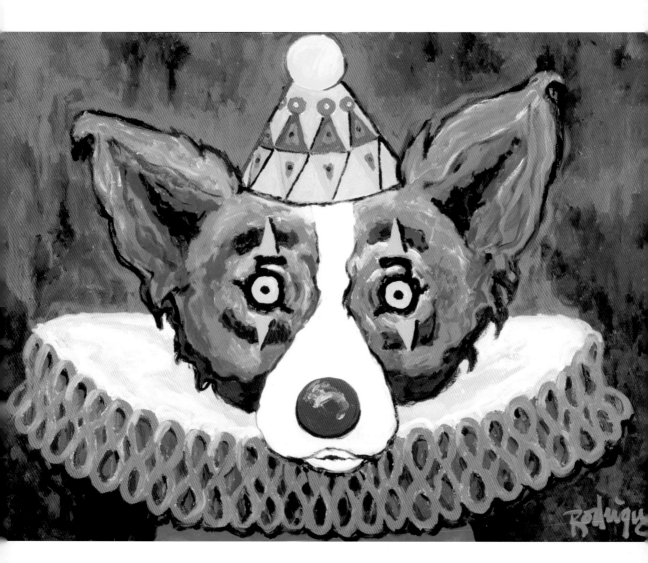

High

I Was a King in   Places

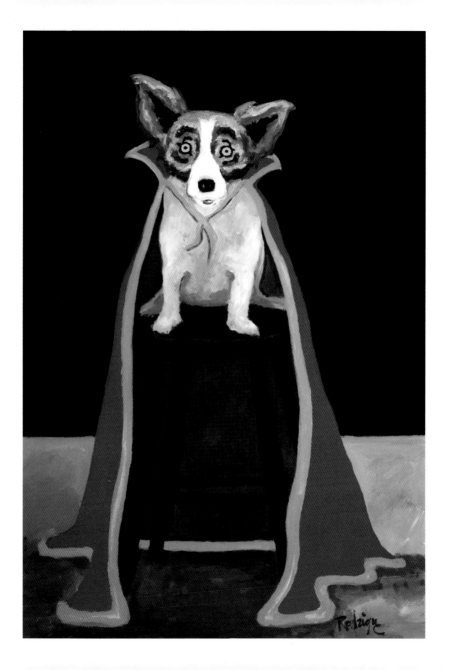

Jester

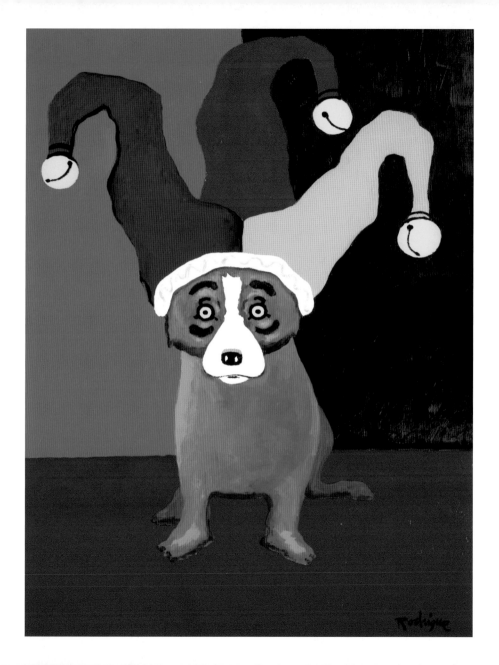

399

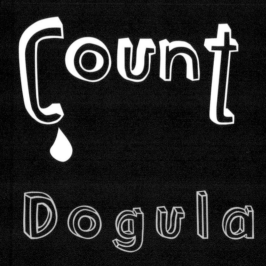

My Hero, Count Dogula

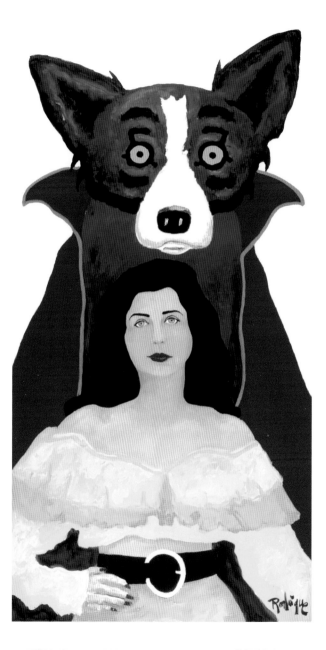

Justice

Power

and

Faith

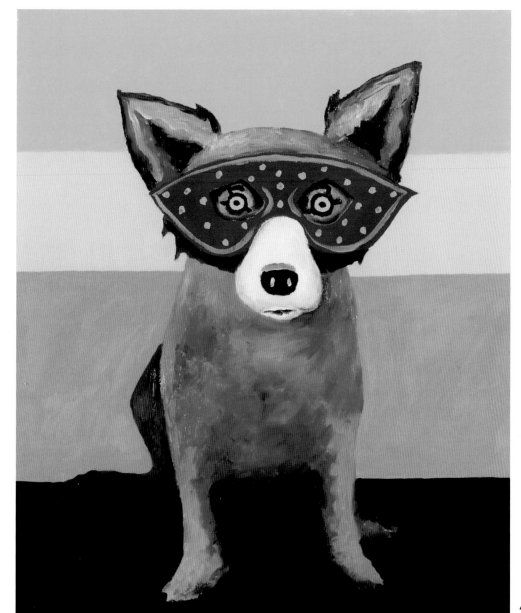

403

Phantom

Dog

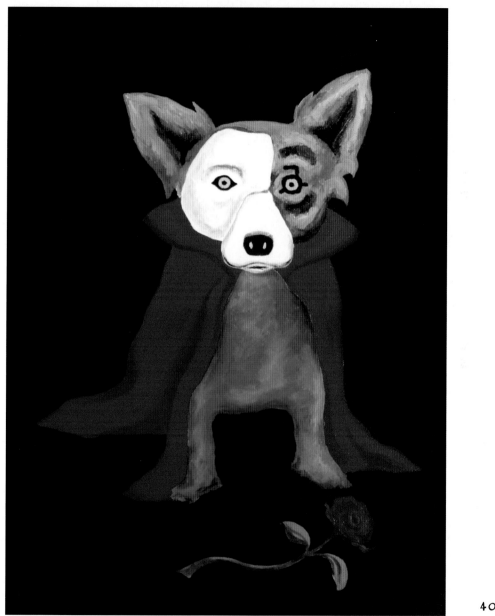

405

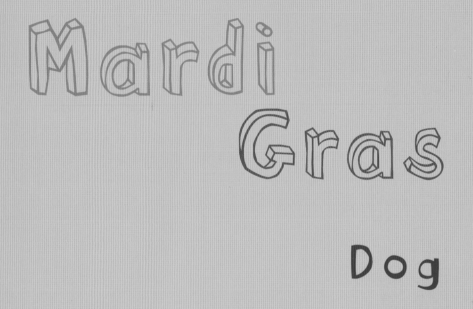

Mardi
Gras

Dog

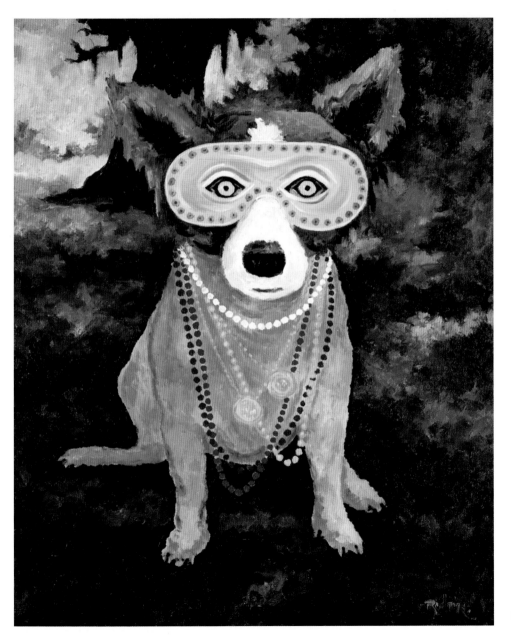

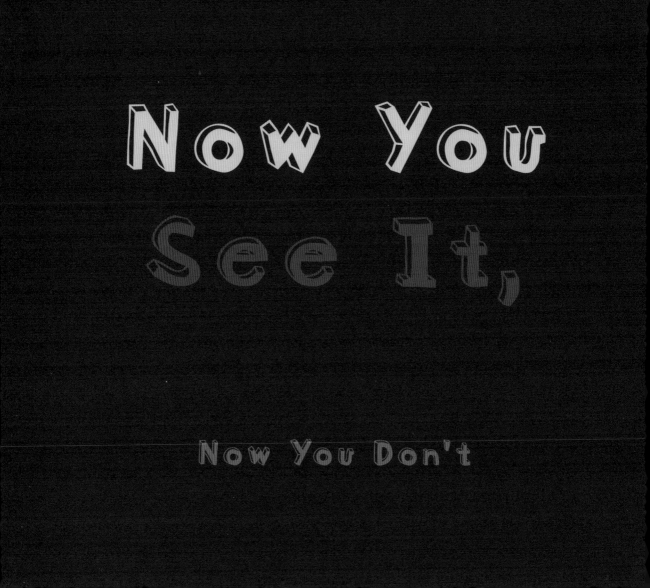

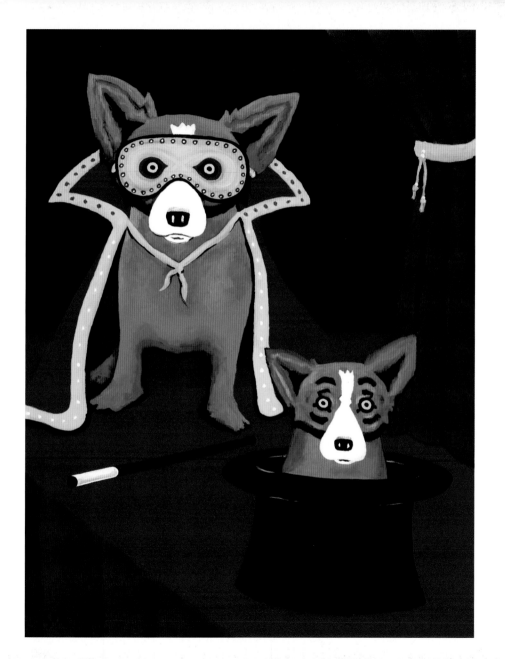

409

10
At Home
with the
Blues

When My Baby Left Me,
All She Left Me Was My Blue Suede Shoes

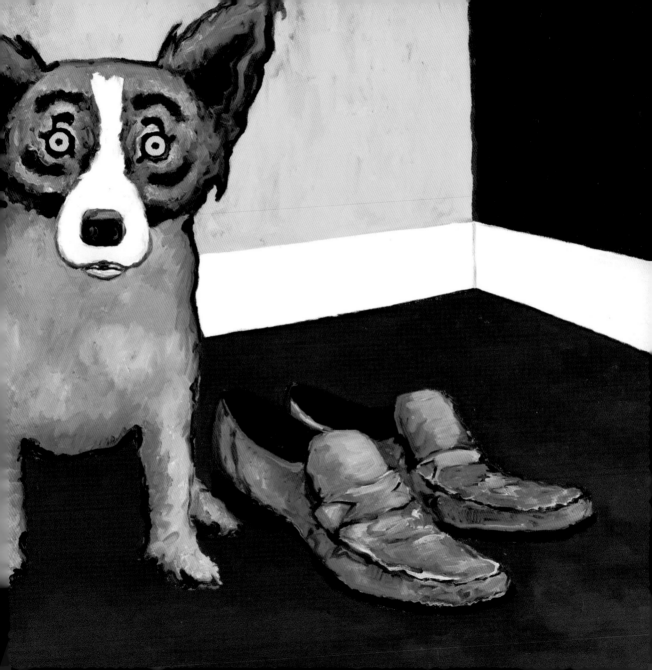

I Proved My Love
for You with
Credit Cards,

But You Were Only
Window-shopping

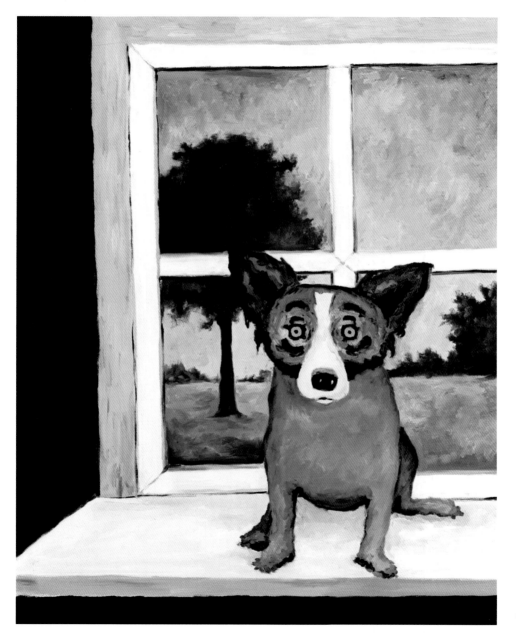

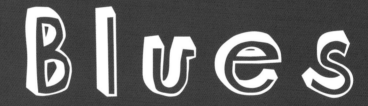

Hiding from the

Blues

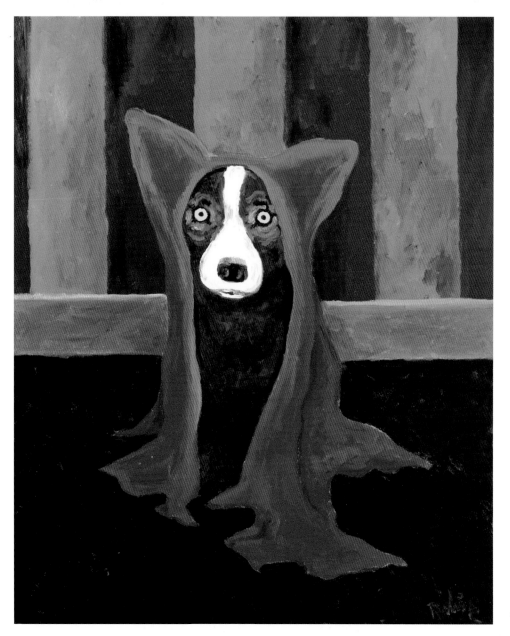

415

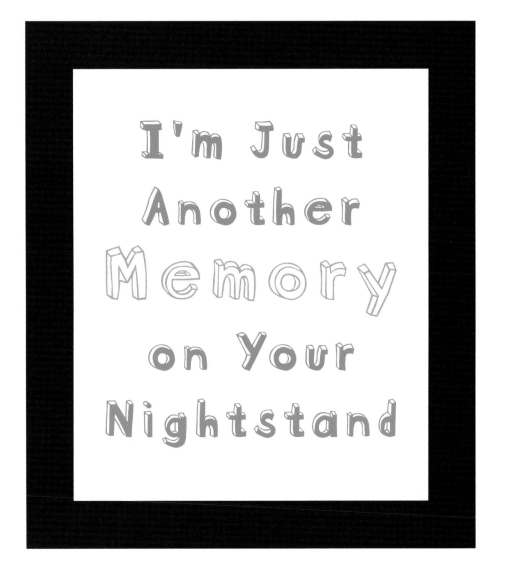

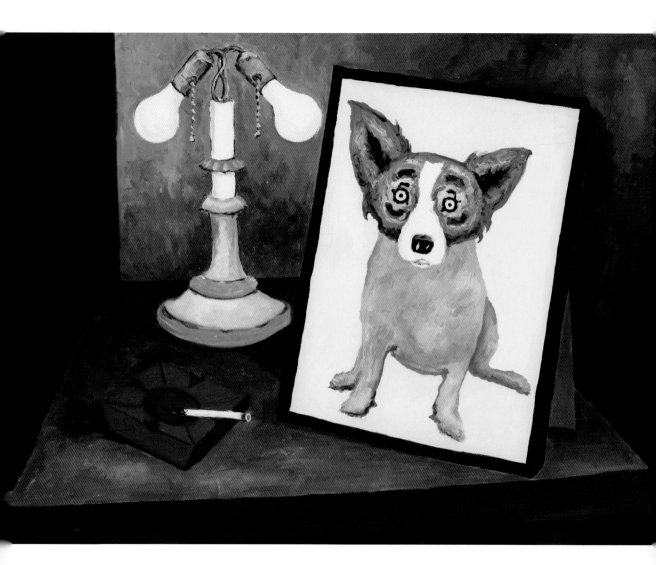

A

Smarter

Breed

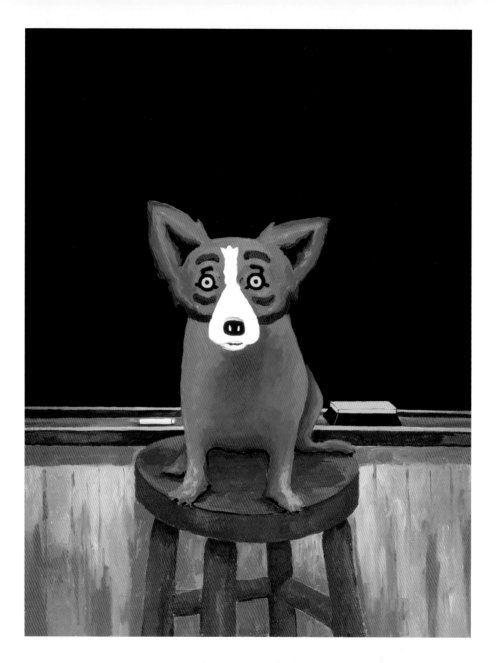

419

I Once
Debated
Nixon

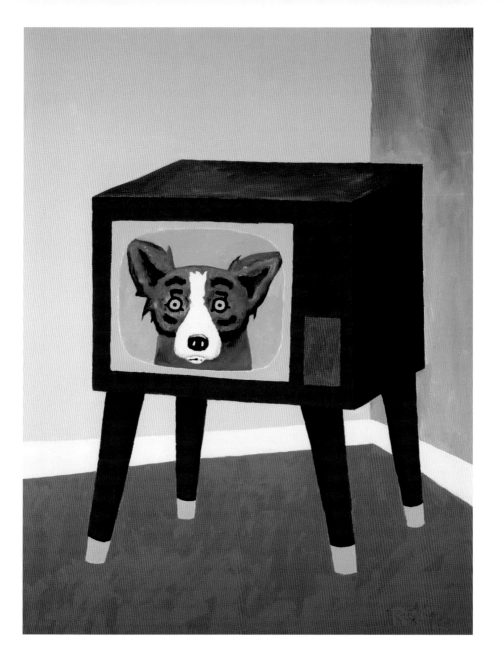

421

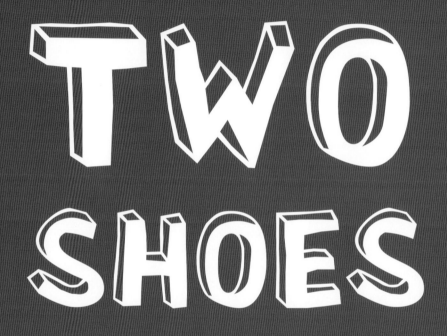

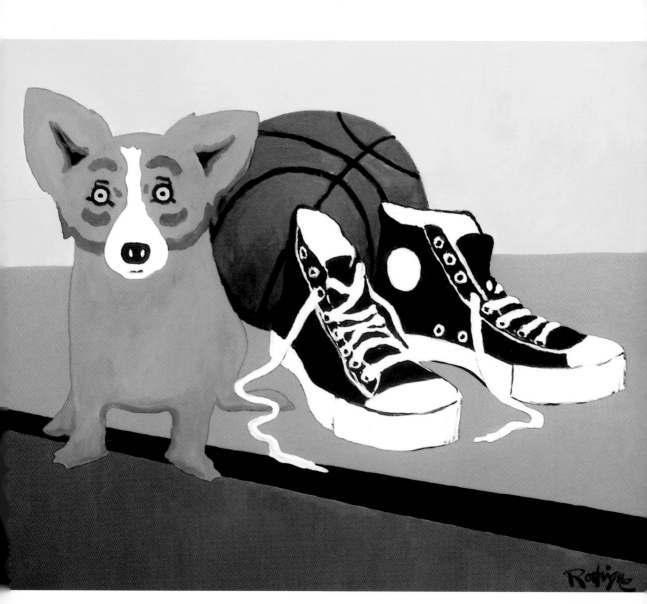

423

My Yellow Chair

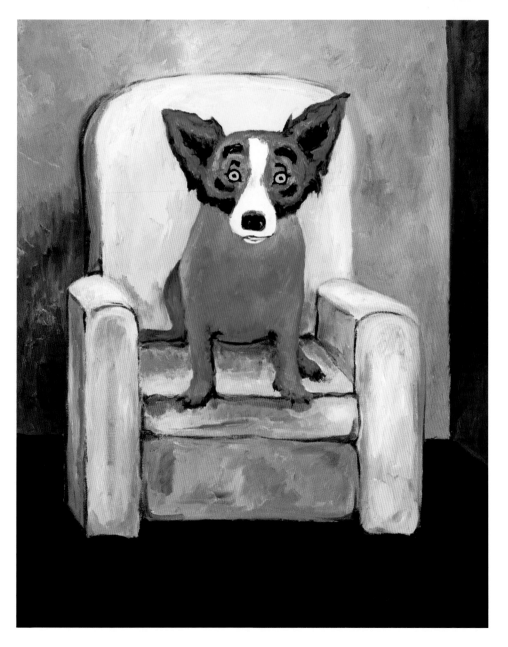

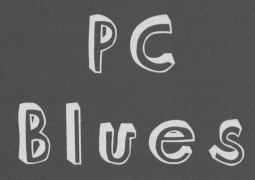

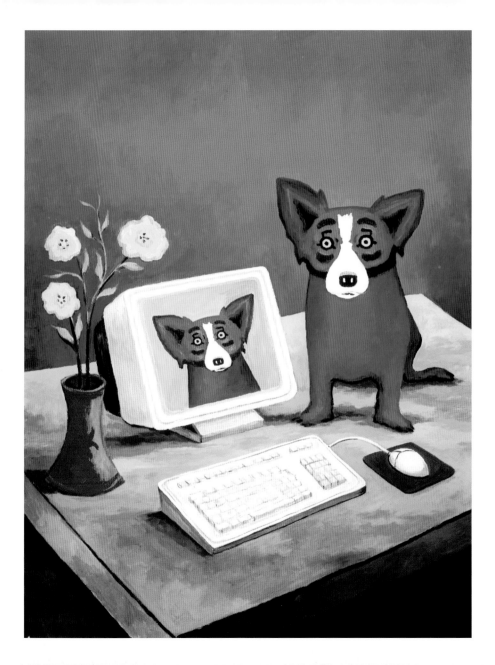

427

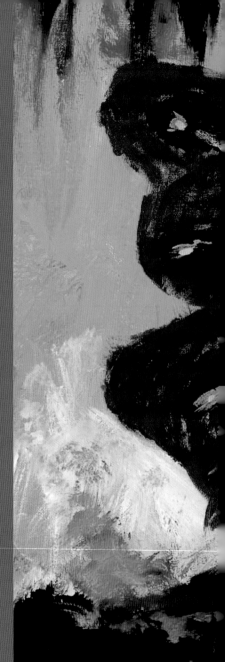

11

On the Road

Breaux Bridge Shoefly

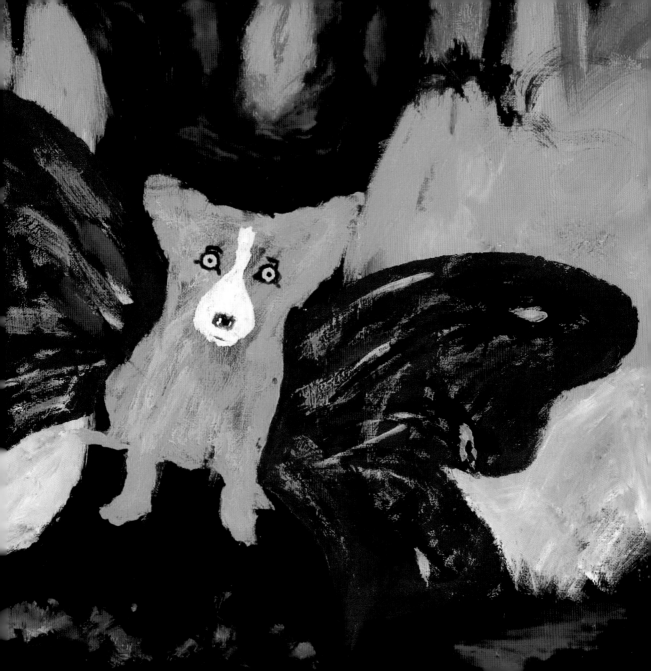

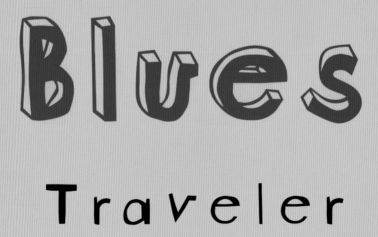

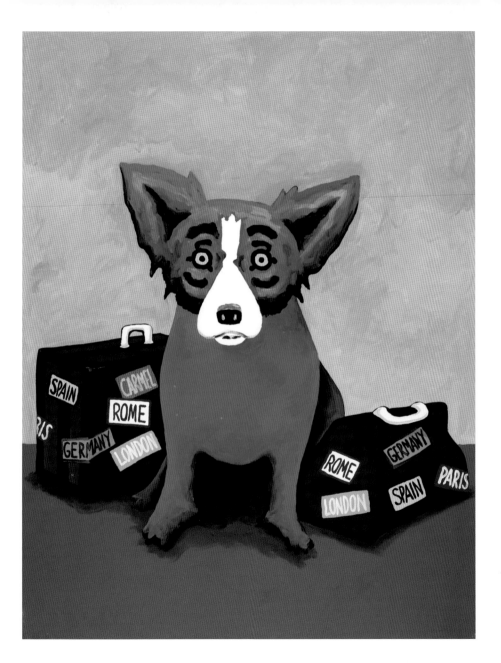

431

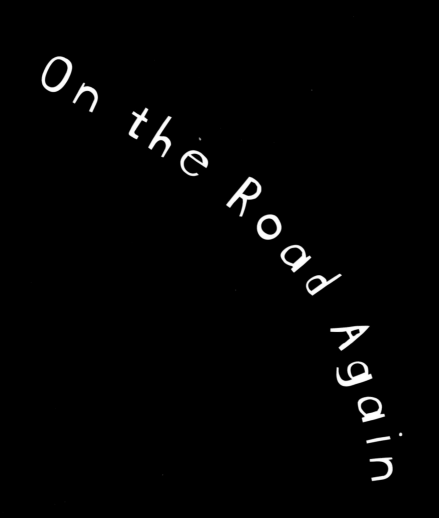

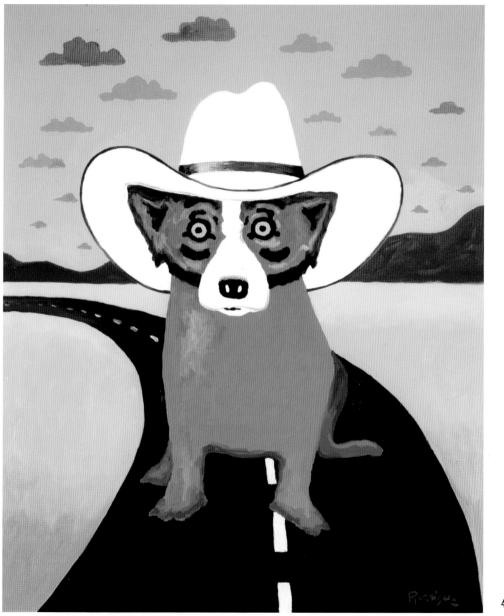

433

The Free Life

(A faster breed)

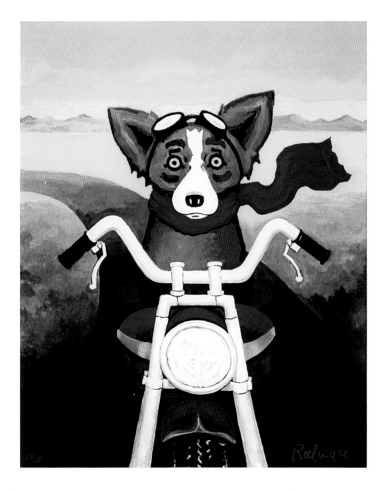

435

My Favorite Part of Town

of Town

(I'm Just Waiting for My Turn)

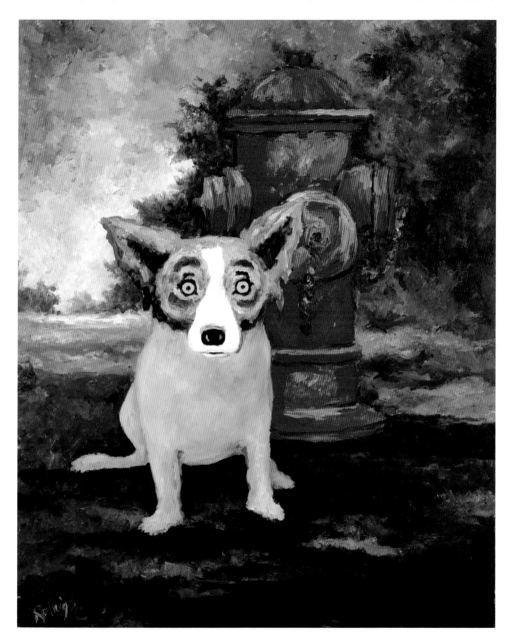

The High Country

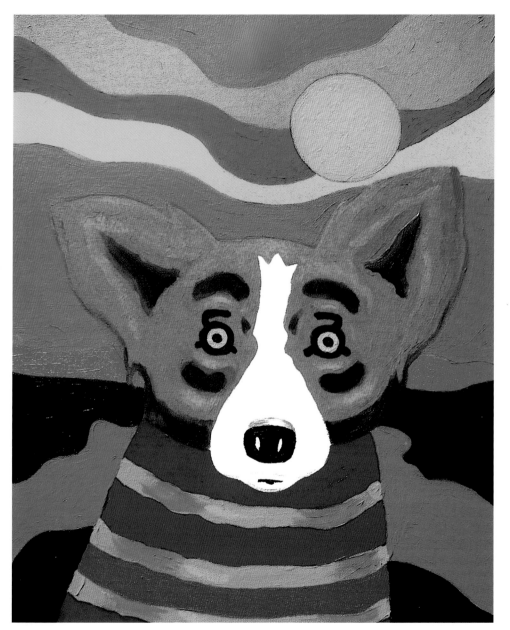

Guess Who's Coming to Dinner

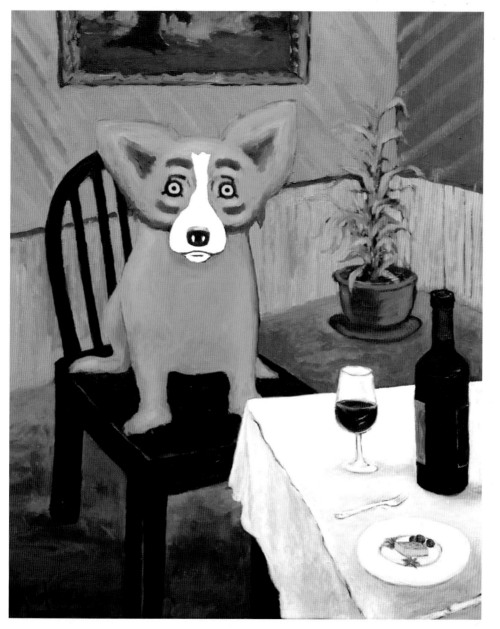

441

Jackpot

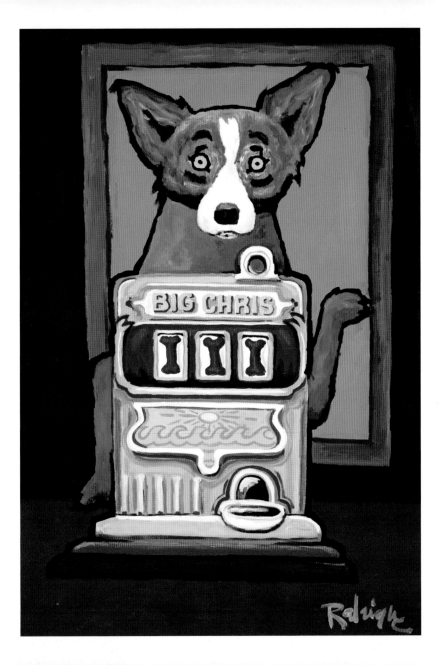

443

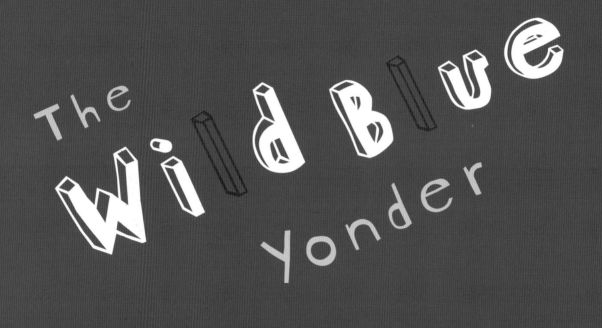

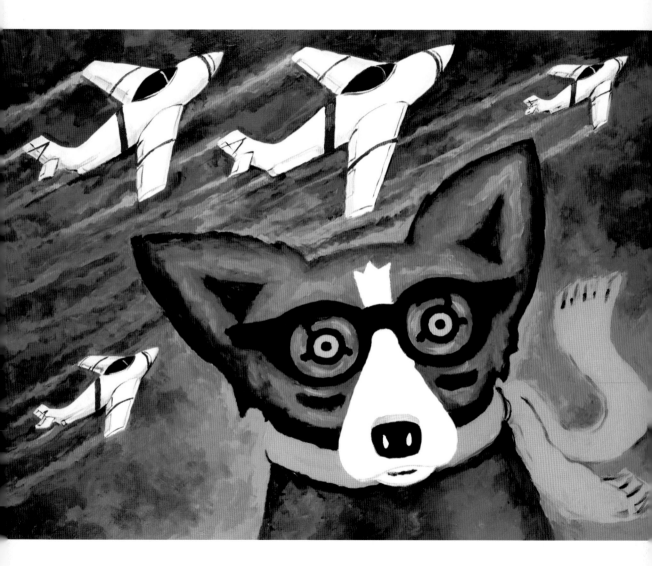

445

Life's a Blast

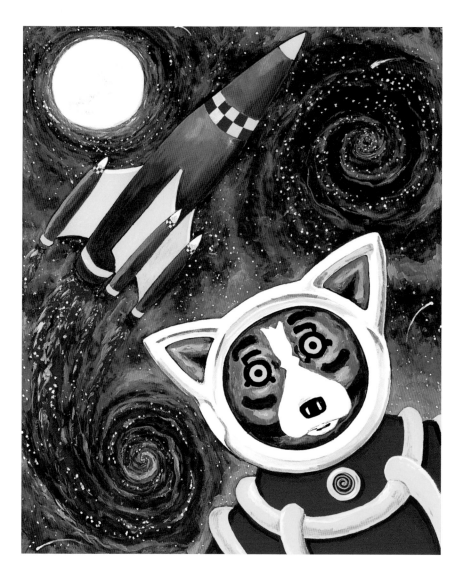

Star-
Hopping
(Export Business)

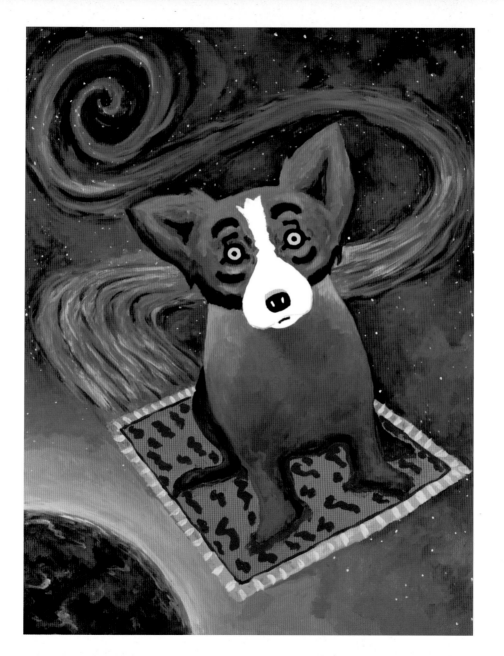

449

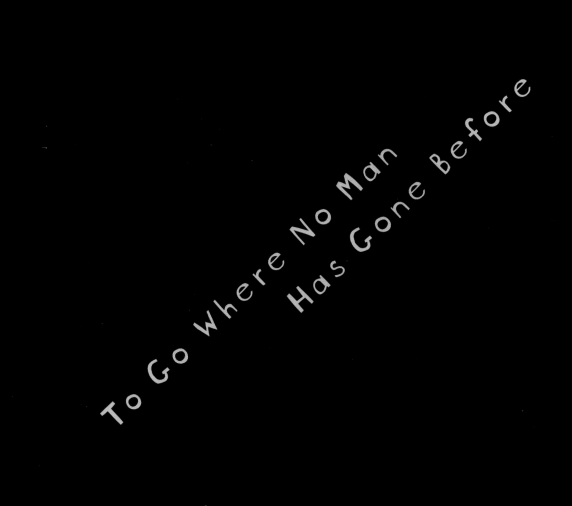

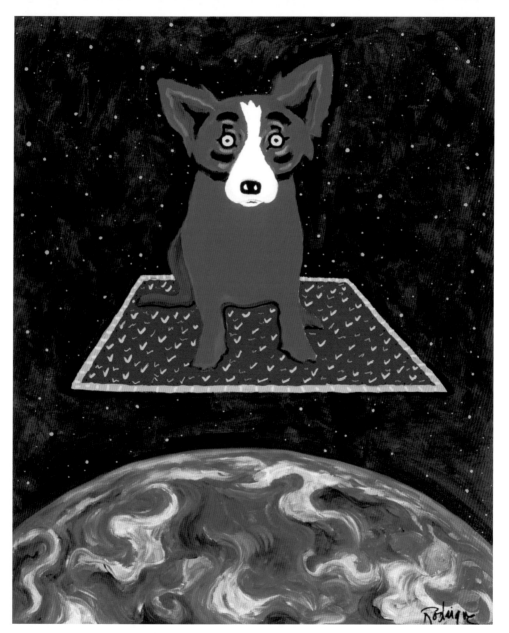

451

12
Taking Care of Business

My Blues Brothers

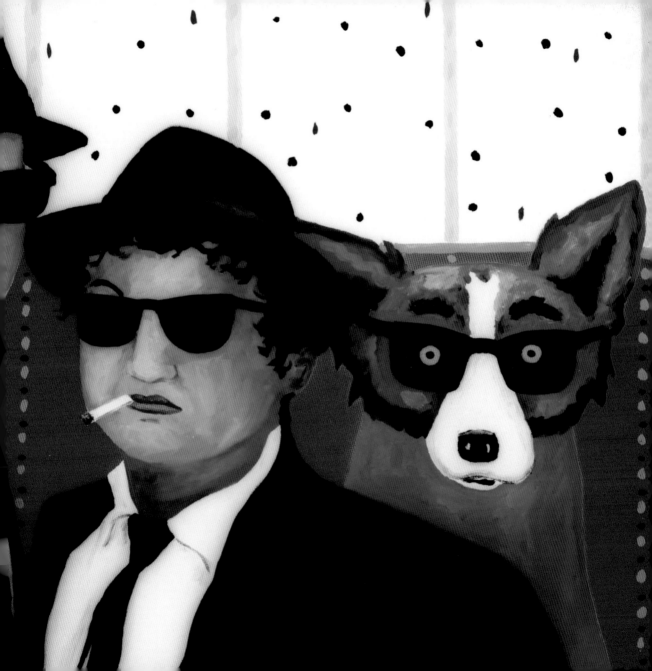

Big Night

Tonight

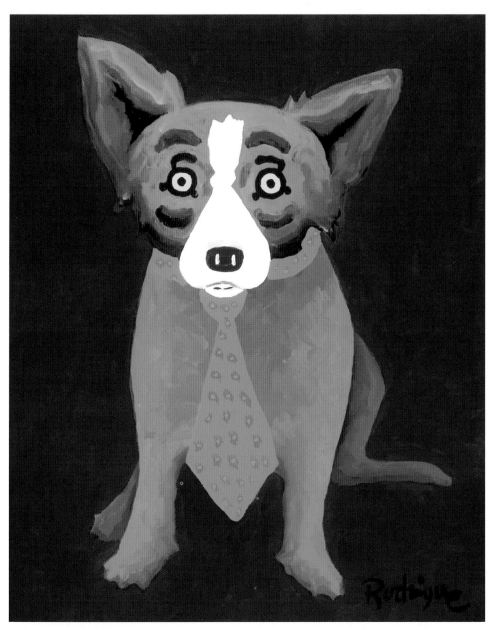

455

Hot Tubbin'

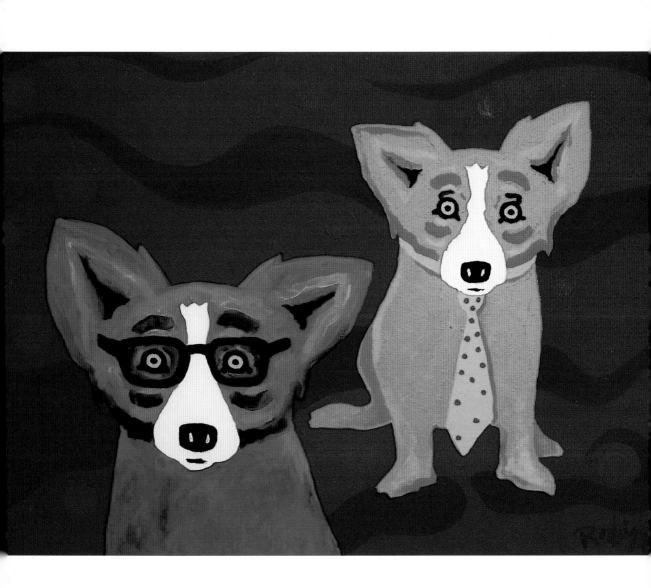

457

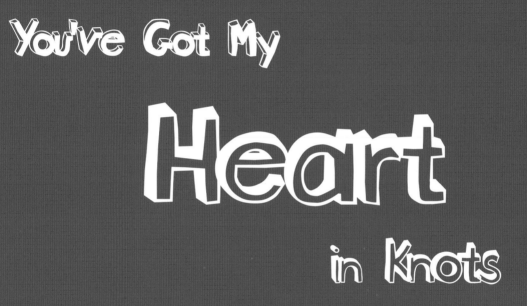

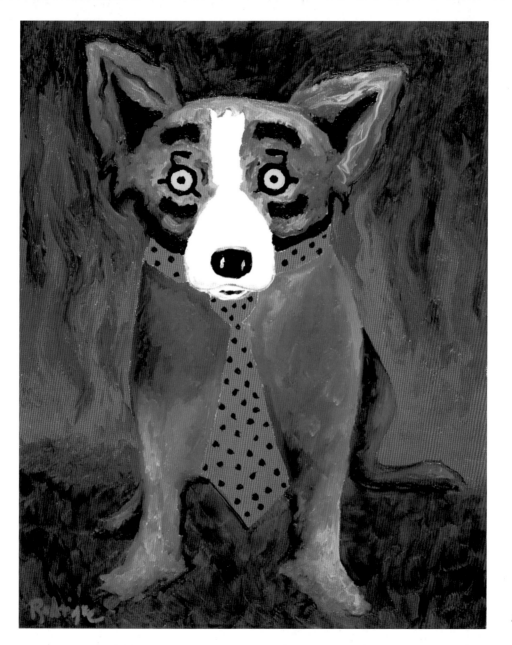

459

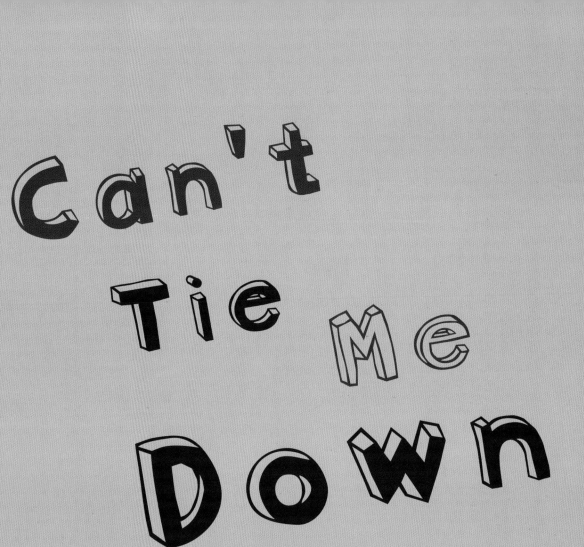

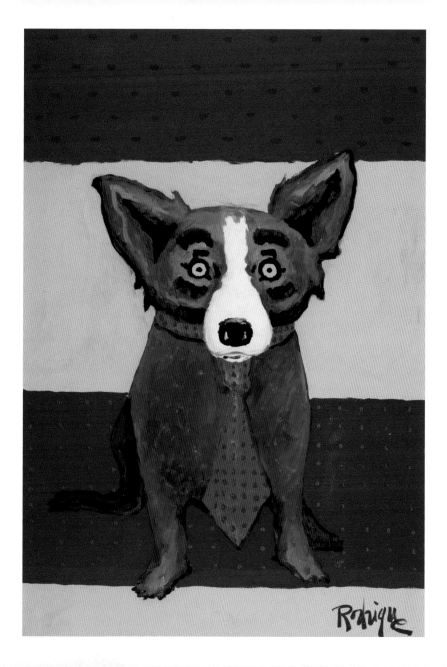

Don't

Tie

Me

Down

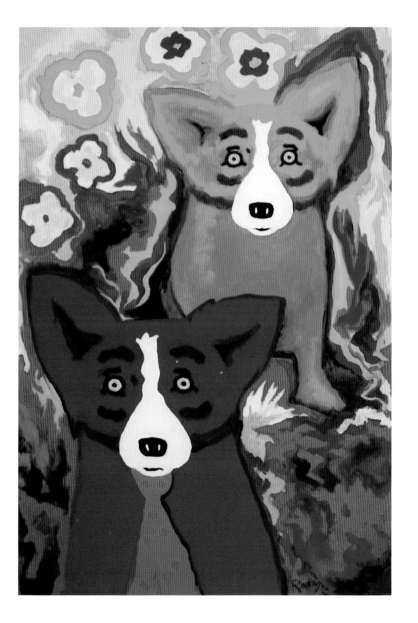

463

I Ain't No

Cartoon

Dog

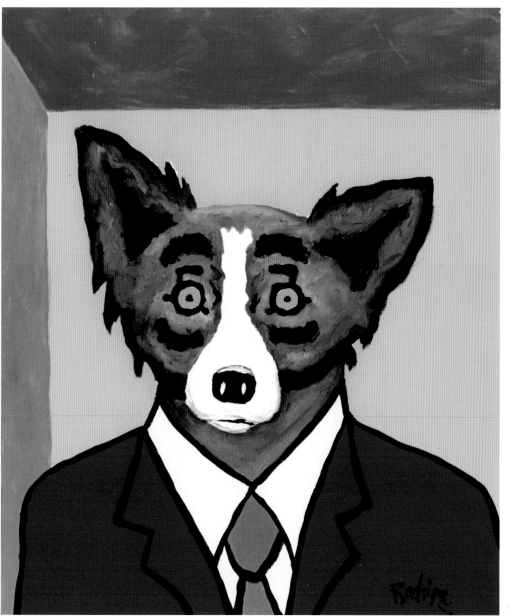

465

Secret

Service

Dog

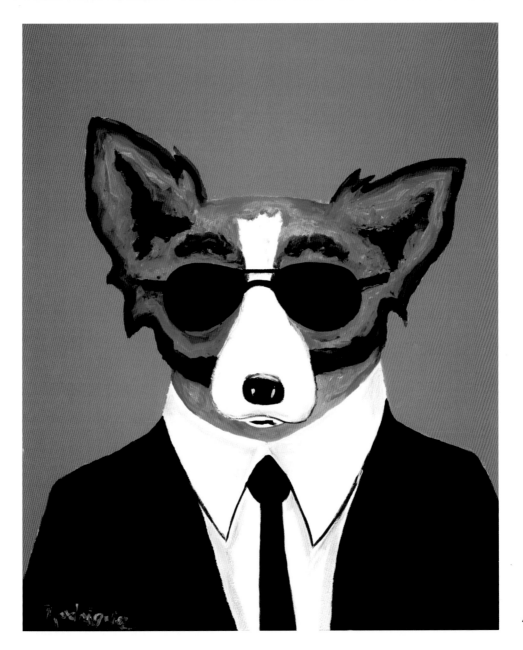

467

Yuppie Puppy

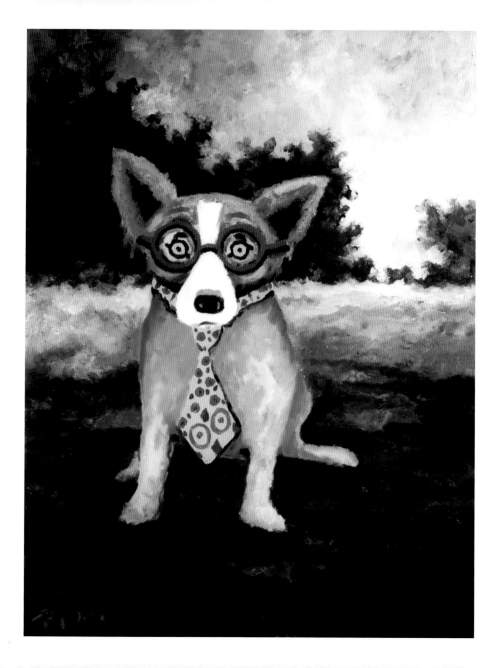

469

Wall

Street

Blues

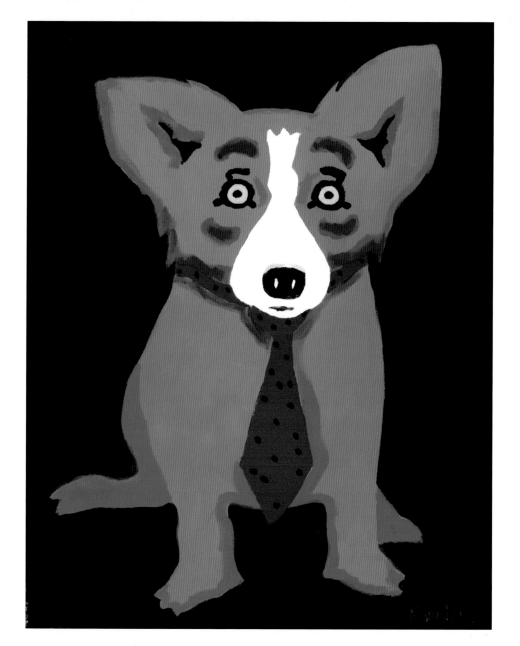

471

We Make Money
the Old-
Fashioned
Way

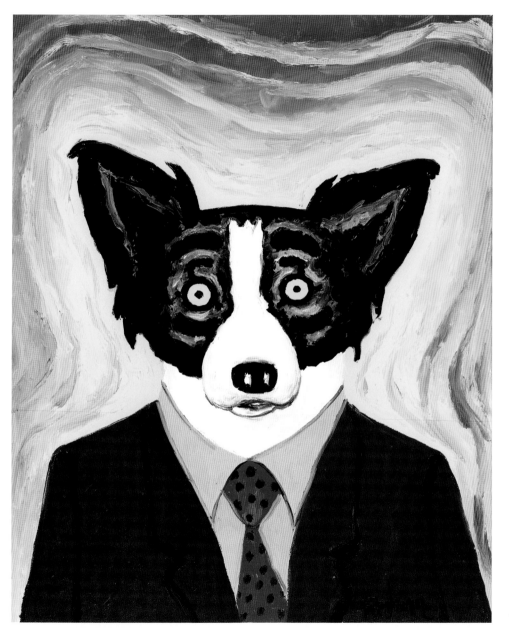

473

13

Hurricane

You Can't Drown the Blues

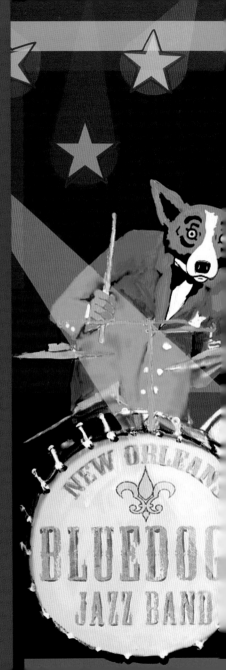

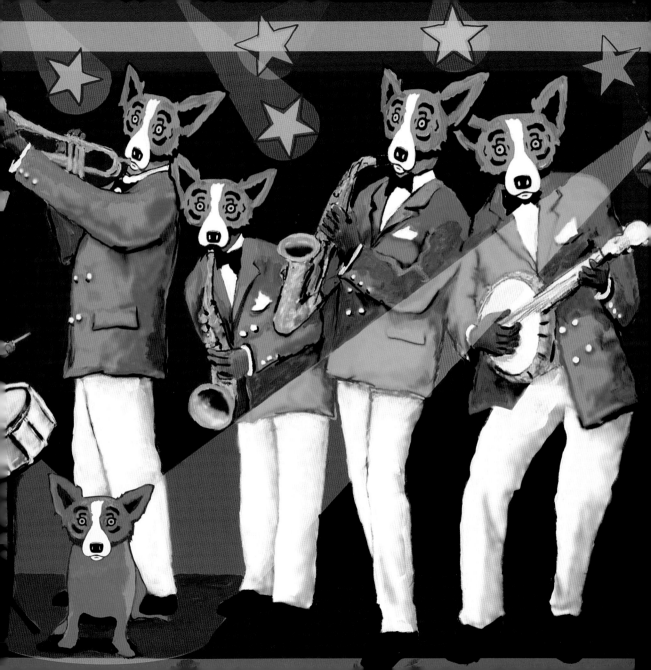

We Will Rise Again

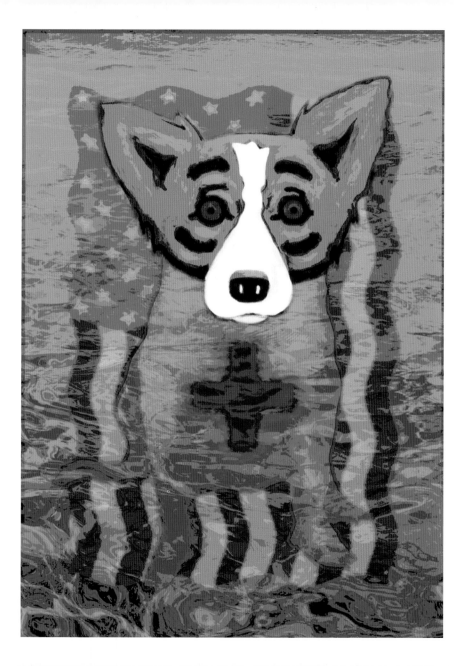

477

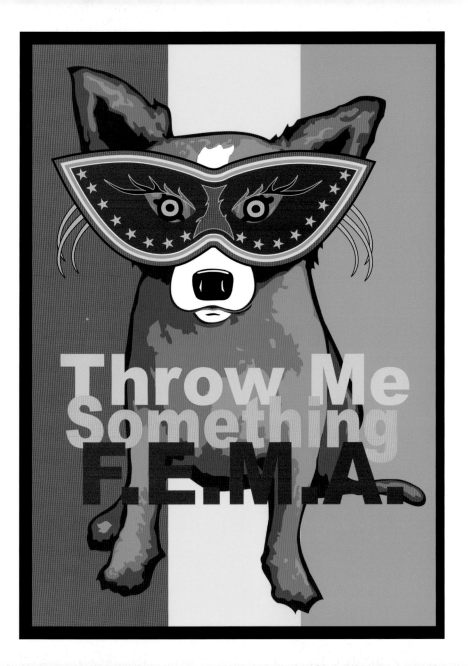

479

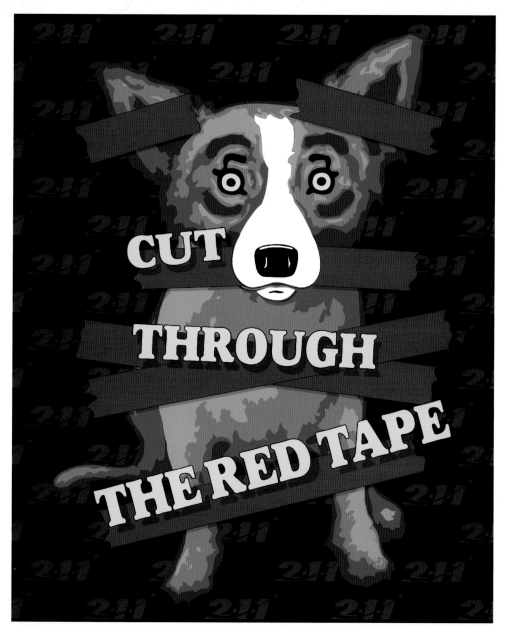

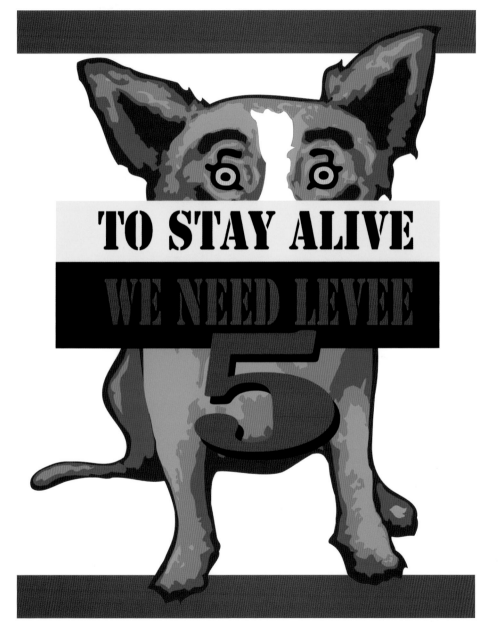

483

We Are Marching Again

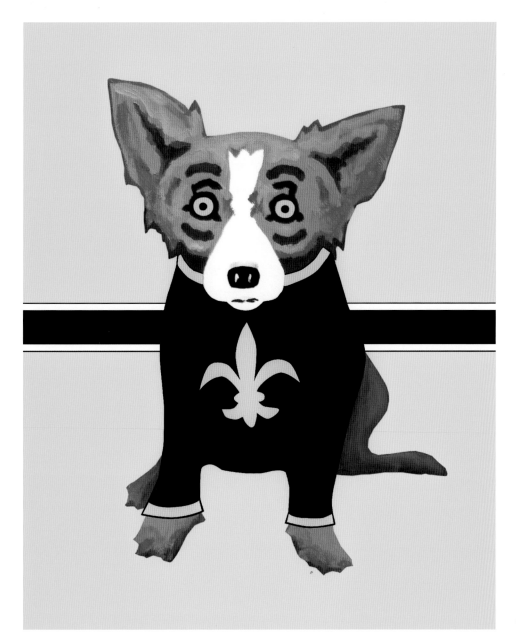

485

14
Red,
White, and
Blue

Paul Revere

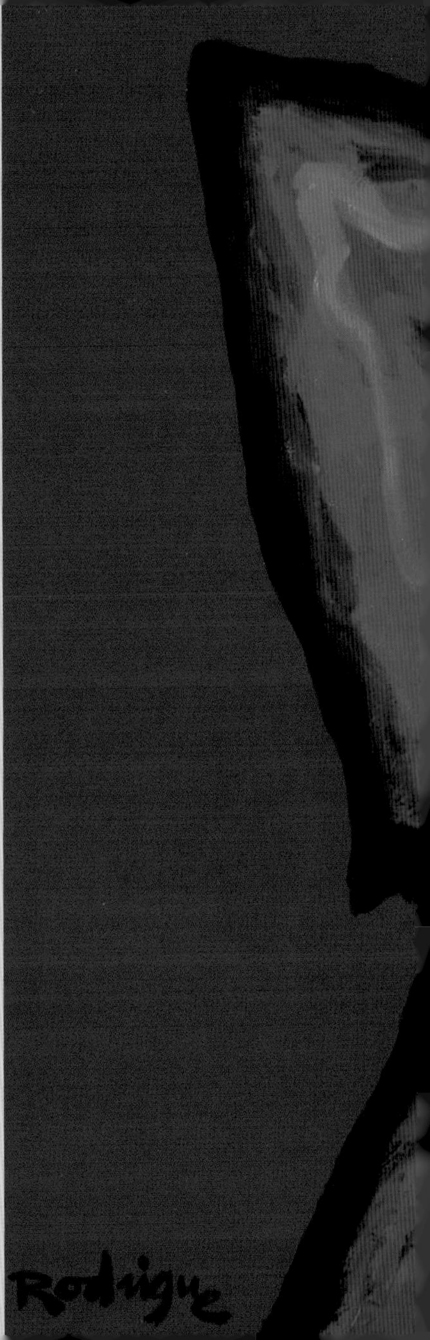

Rodrigue

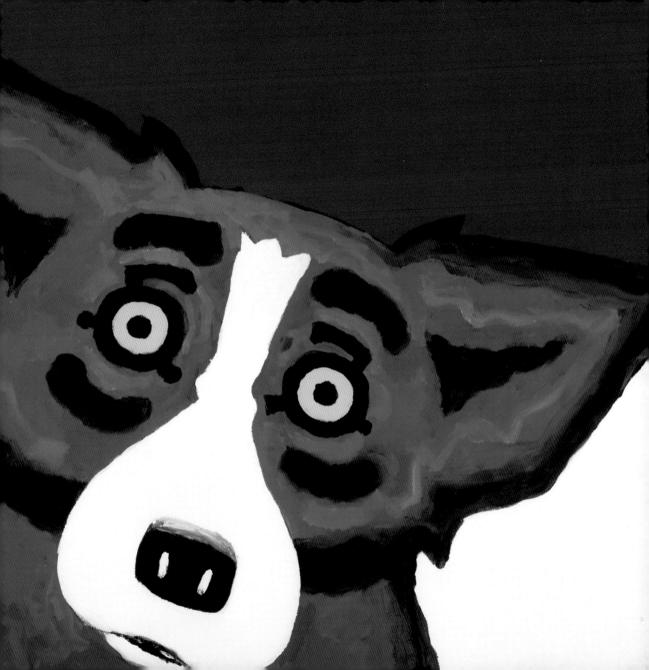

As Honest as the Day Is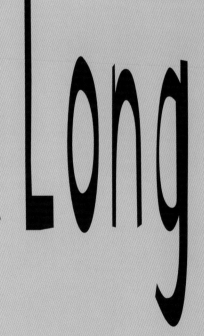

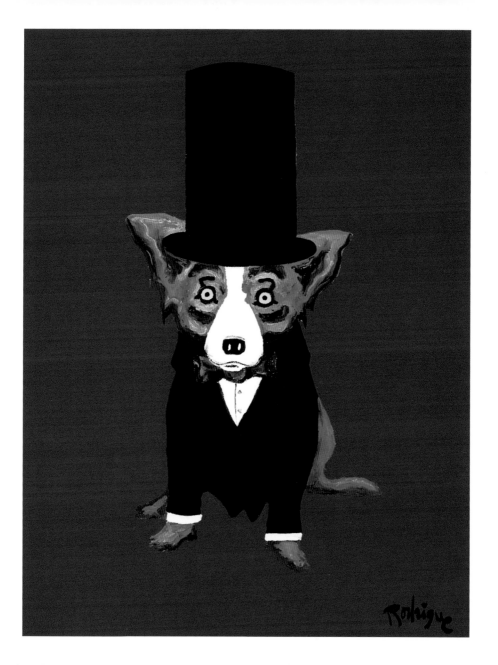

489

God Bless
America

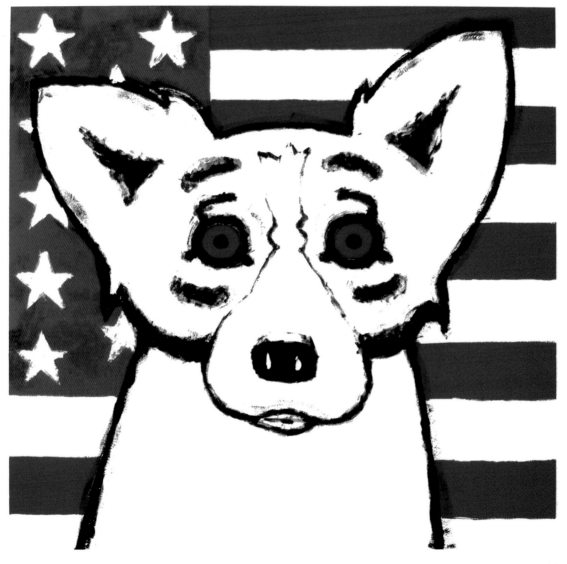

491

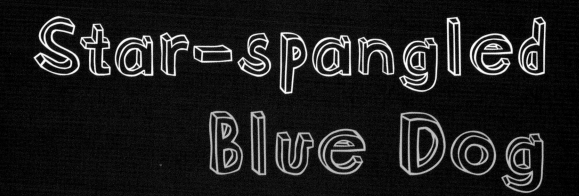

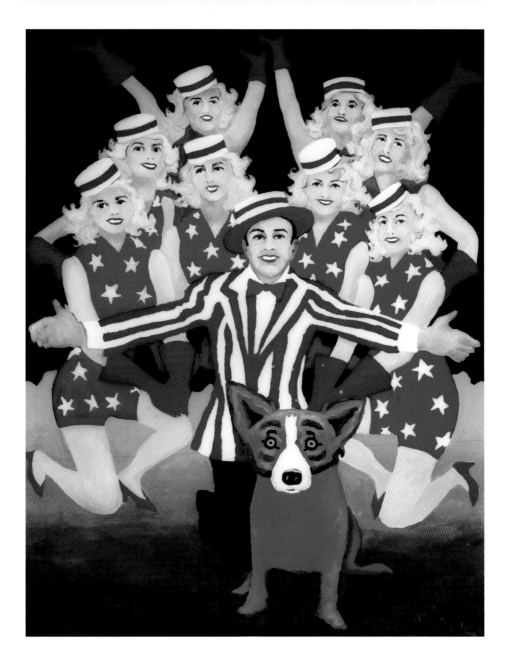

493

Star

Rising

Catch a

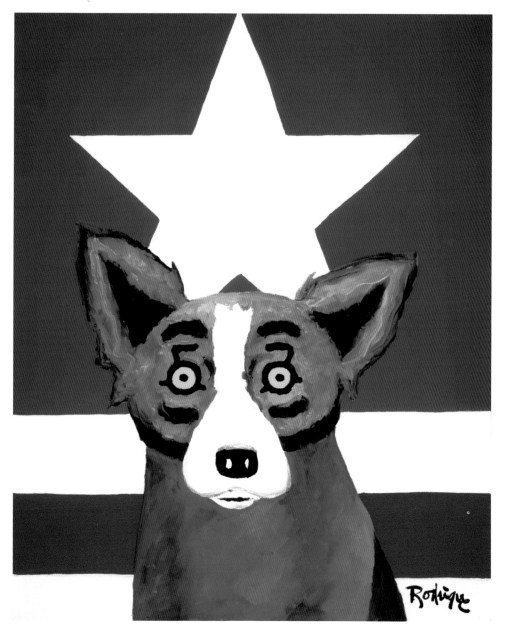

495

I Live for
My Country

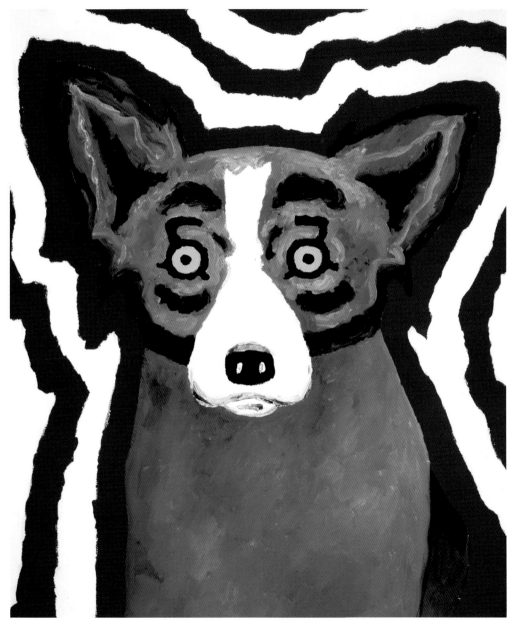

497

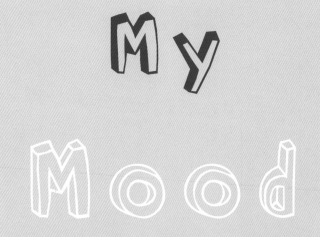

My Mood Changes

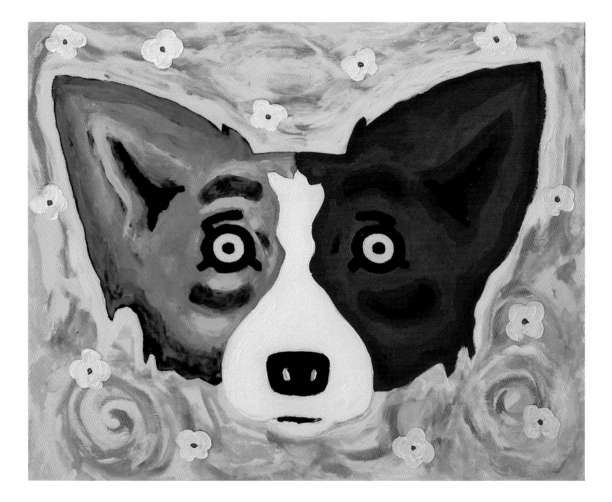

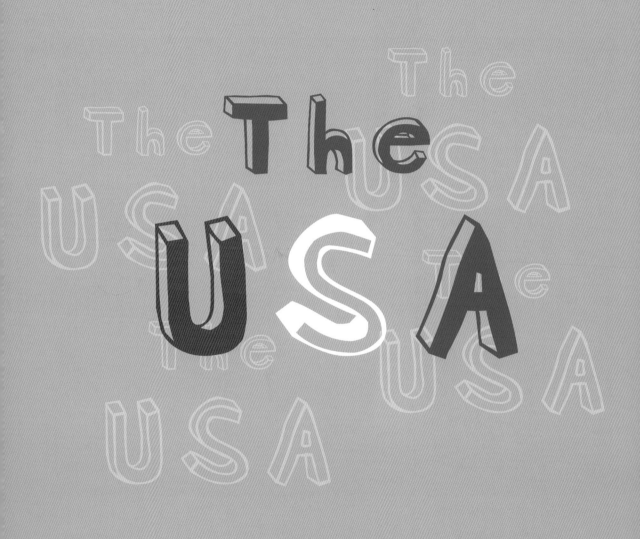

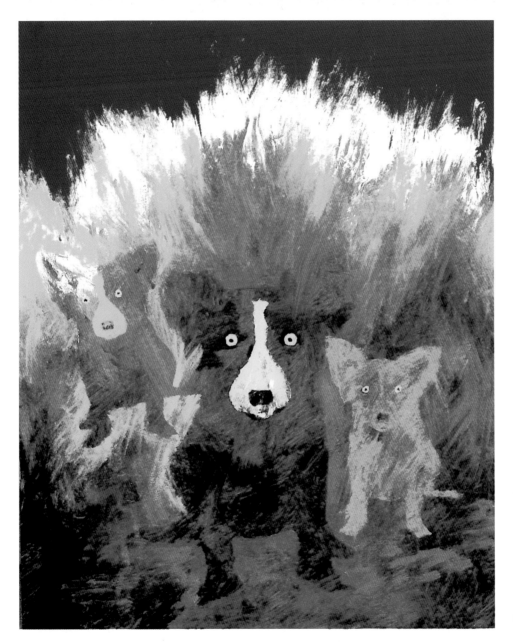

501

Stars & Stripes & Me

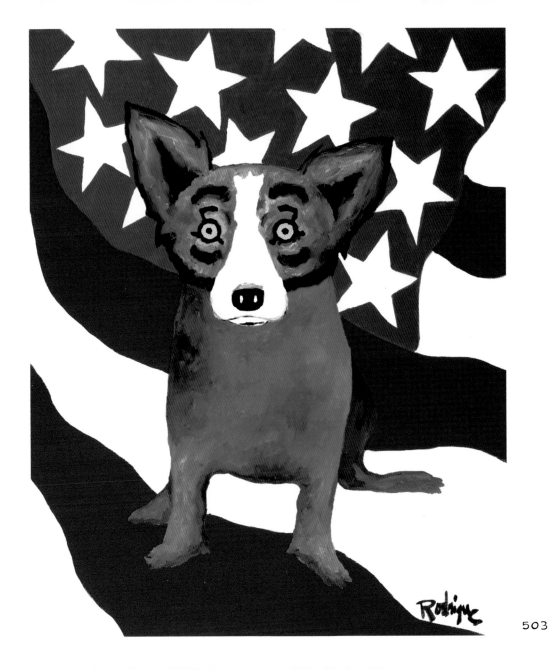

503

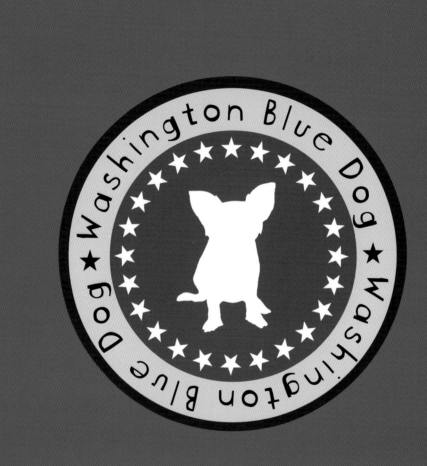

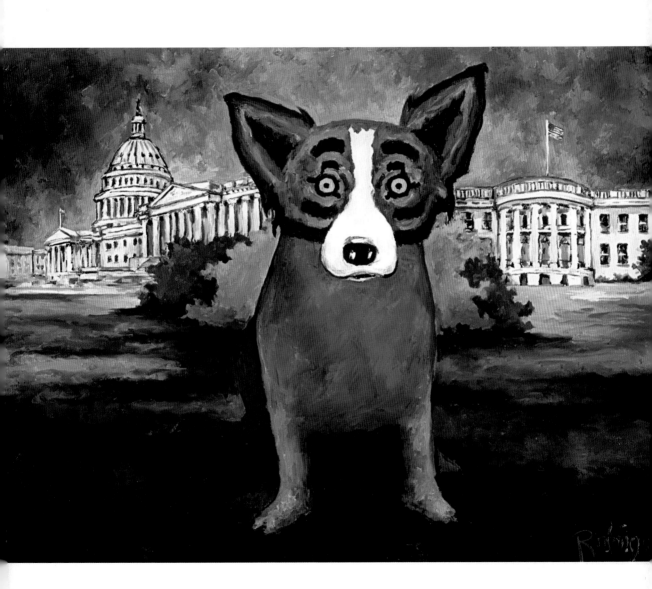

505

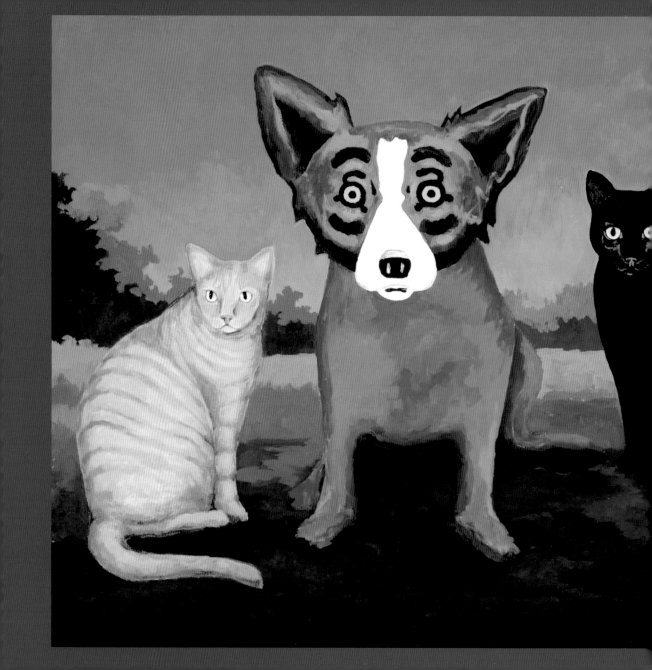

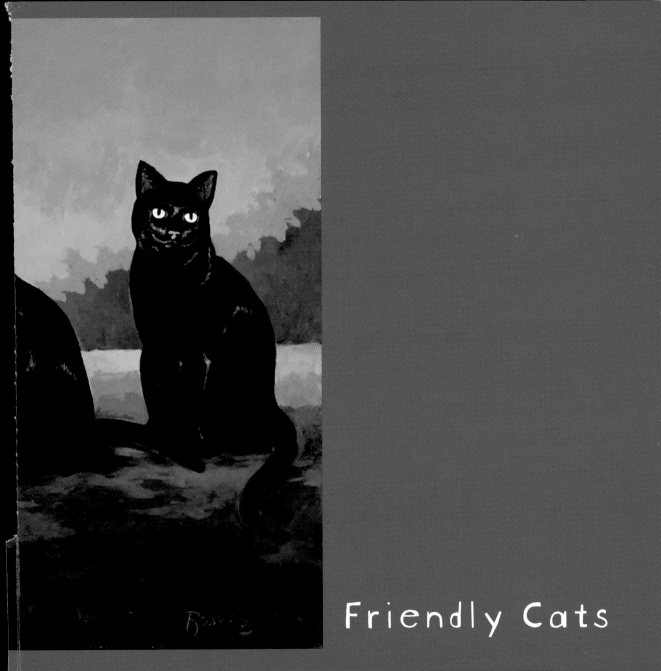

Friendly Cats

INDEX